# This Call May Be Monitored

# This Call May Be Monitored

## What Eavesdropping on Corporate America Taught Me About Business and Life

## Tom Vander Well

### The Man in the Middle™

Expert Press
1067 N Main Street #235
Nicholasville, KY 40356
www.ExpertPress.net

Editing by Valerie Denor
Copyediting by Lucy Spencer
Proofreading by Heather Dubnick
Text design and composition by Emily Fritz
Cover design by Casey Fritz

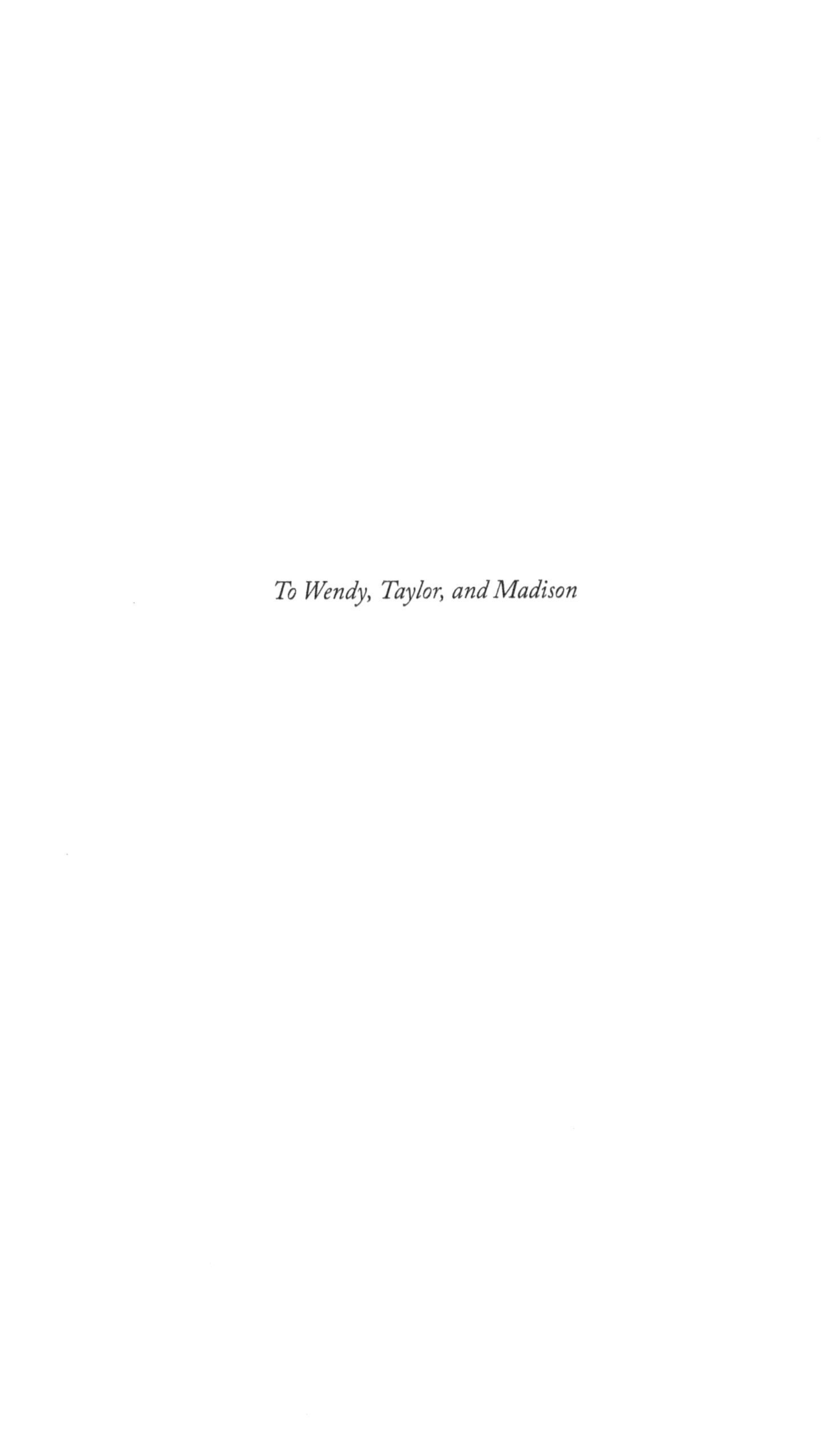

*To Wendy, Taylor, and Madison*

# Acknowledgments

The seeds of this book were planted at the Peanut Pub in Pella, Iowa, many years ago, as I sipped a pint and journaled all the life lessons my career had afforded me. Turning it into a book was a dream that took years to become a reality.

I'd like to thank Chuck and Charleen Wenger and all my colleagues at c wenger group and Intelligentics through the years. Thanks also to Scott Wier, Bené Zehr, and Matthew Burch, who were special companions on the journey.

I want to express my gratitude to all our clients through the years who entrusted me and my colleagues with the opportunity to serve. You gave me far more than a paycheck. This book is a witness to that.

Thank you to Michael DeLon and the team at Paperback Expert for being the right people at the right time to turn this dream into a reality. Special thanks to Valerie Denor for sharing with me her expertise, her story, and her heart.

# Contents


**Section 1: The Man in the Middle** — 1

1   How I Found Myself Stuck in the Middle — 5

2   Foundations of Quality Assessment (QA) — 31

**Section 2: The Front Line of Business** — 55

3   Quality — 59

4   How Call Monitoring and QA Work — 93

5   Motivation and Morale — 135

**Section 3: At the Top** — 161

6   Leadership for the Service Excellence Journey — 163

7   Lessons from the Trenches — 181

8   The Last Call — 199

About the Author — 207

# The Man in the Middle

I have personally assessed and analyzed over 100,000 phone calls between businesses and their customers since 1994. I have listened to calls for every imaginable transaction, including quotes, orders, tech support, billing, complaints, compliments, and even threats. My clients have been both business-to-customer (B2C) and business-to-business (B2B). They include every kind of company: finance, retailers, automakers, home shopping networks, catalog companies, and sporting goods.

I've heard sales and support calls for manufacturers and distributors of heatsink pads, industrial adhesives, circuit boards, and every electronic component imaginable. Insurance, playground equipment, memberships, hospitality, industrial equipment, health care, and government services are all industries I've monitored.

My wiretapping privileges have reached far beyond sales and service trades. I've analyzed simple collection calls with customers who missed a payment on their lawn tractors. I've analyzed hour-long collection calls with customers who defaulted on millions of dollars in loans. I've prayed silent prayers for people I don't even know as I listened to real people share horrific tragedies that led to them not being able to make their mortgage payment.

I've spent my career eavesdropping on companies of all shapes and sizes. I've been privileged to serve global corporations and major brands like John Deere, Volvo, Principal Financial, and Cabela's. I've been even more honored to serve smaller private and family-owned businesses you've never heard of. My smallest client was a guy who provided inside sales from his desk inside what had been a janitor's closet. A decade later, he was managing six inside agents as our team helped his company succeed and grow.

The founder of my company, Intelligentics, was a man named Chuck Wenger. When he started the company in 1987, it was called c wenger group because it began as a partnership between Chuck and his wife, Charleen. When Chuck hired me in 1994, it wasn't because I had knowledge or experience in call monitoring or quality assessment (QA). No one did. QA was just emerging as a trending discipline in business.

Instead, Chuck summarized the job qualifications. He explained that someone had to be the man in the middle. "I need someone who can tell front-line customer service representatives (CSRs) making minimum wage what the data says, and train them to improve. Then, the same person must meet with the CEO to discuss what the data means for the tactical strategy of the entire business."

To this day, I question Chuck's sanity, but he hired me for the job. I've had a unique career that has afforded me the quirky opportunity to see and examine business from an eclectic perspective.

In his best-selling book *Outliers*, Malcolm Gladwell wrote that a genius is simply someone who put in the 10,000 hours needed to become an expert. I'm an outlier. I've put in those 10,000 hours analyzing and assessing phone calls to learn what they reveal about a business and their customers' experiences.

Most people have not had the chance to observe so many businesses from this perspective. Most business gurus diagnose the headaches from the brains of the C-suite. Not me. I'm the man with a proctoscope invading the front-line contact center where the fecal matter comes into direct contact with the electric rotary oscillator of customer experience.

Every phone call is a moment of truth in which the business can either win or lose a customer. I have done a forensic deep dive into tens of thousands of moments of truth. In every call I've analyzed, the customer walked away from the experience with either an enhanced or diminished perception of our client.

I have learned a host of lessons about business and life by examining each moment of truth from a customer's perspective. The lessons I learned over the decades now rest between your fingertips.

I freely give you my life's work for two reasons. First, I want to help you succeed in your business. Many lessons are profound in their simplicity, but some of the deepest truths are so simple that we overlook them.

The second purpose of this book is even more important to me: I want to help you succeed in life. When I entered this career, I never expected I would learn so many life lessons from what I do every day. Being a call analyst means both helping agents to improve their service and advising managers to improve their teams. It means bridging the cavern between the CSR and the CEO to identify detrimental policies and procedures. All these things have taught me lessons I've also applied to marriage, parenting, relationships, faith, and my personal life journey.

Before I ever sat between CSRs and CEOs or listened to my first recorded call, I found myself standing at a very different crossroads, one that shaped how I would listen, lead, and live for the rest of my life. Before I tell you about my business, I want to tell you my story.

# CHAPTER 1

# How I Found Myself Stuck in the Middle

Lisa is my friend and colleague. She is a wonderful individual who looks at life in interesting ways. She once decided not to buy groceries until she ate every item in her kitchen to see how long she could endure before going shopping. On another occasion, Lisa asked everyone, "Does your life look like you expected it would when you were young?" Not one person she asked answered "Yes."

Do your life and career look like you expected? When you were in high school, what did you envision you would spend your 10,000 hours doing? How's that worked out for you? Yeah, me too.

I never expected to become a business analyst of recorded phone calls. To be honest, I never wanted to work in business.

I was dead set on doing something completely different in my life. Instead, I found myself a "man in the middle."

## The Life-Changing Experience

When I was a young teenager, I had a spiritual experience that forever changed my life. I was raised in church, but like many teenagers, the institutional church penetrated my heart like water sinks into a river rock. I was your typical self-centered, insecure teenage boy making stupid decisions.

I was a high school freshman when a senior asked me to join her at a church for live music and a speaker. I jumped at the chance to go. Honestly, I wasn't that interested in the meetings; I was interested in the girl. She was cute, and she was a senior. As the old saying goes, "The Lord works in mysterious ways."

The song "Amazing Grace" contains a line about the experience of being blind and receiving sight. The first night of the weekend was a spiritually eye-opening experience. I had heard about Jesus my entire life. I knew all the Sunday school stories. I even got the confirmation certificate with the accompanying box of offering envelopes.

But all those things did not make any real difference in my life.

After the message, I walked down the aisle, got down on my knees, and prayed a simple prayer. I surrendered all that I am to Jesus. I asked Him to be Lord of my life, and I committed to live for Him. Whatever He wanted.

Wherever He led. I can't explain it, but at that moment everything changed.

I went home and told my sister she had to accompany us to the meeting the following night. That night, two even more amazing things happened. First, my sister walked down the aisle, kneeled down, and prayed her own prayer of surrender.

As my sister gave her life to Christ, my own prayer was accompanied by a vision. It feels strange even typing those words. For a moment, it felt like everything around me receded and I was inside a dream. I was preaching from the platform of the church. Then I heard a voice say, "You're going to proclaim my Word."

That was it. I realize that sounds really silly to many people.

I went home and told my parents that I thought God wanted me to become a minister. Mom was folding laundry. Dad was lying on the couch watching television. They were a bit shocked by my sudden pronouncement.

Their shock morphed into bewilderment as they witnessed changes in my sister and me. We didn't fight anymore. We complained less. We obeyed more. We read and studied the Bible all the time.

I told God that I was happy to comply with His vision, but He would have to arrange things. I was, after all, just shy of my fifteenth birthday. Two months after the vision, my youth group took charge of the Sunday morning service.

I was one of three who were asked to give a message. Less than three months after my vision, I preached my first sermon. But wait—it gets better.

A few months later, some friends of my sister invited her to join their church's youth choir. Every year the choir put together a music program and then traveled around the state performing in churches. The director of the choir asked if I'd be willing to share my story about deciding to follow Jesus during the season-opening performance. I said I'd be happy to do so.

When the performance was over, the choir director approached me. "Young man, God has given you a gift. I'd like you to use that gift. Would you like to travel with us this year? Every time the choir performs, you'll be given fifteen to twenty minutes to deliver a message."

Less than a year after my dream-like vision, I traveled the state preaching in a different church every Sunday. This continued throughout the rest of my high school years. It seemed that my path was set: I was going to be a preacher.

Around the same time, I met Chuck Wenger. Chuck was the vice president of marketing for a local company. There was just something about Chuck. I couldn't put my finger on it at first. Chuck was one of the most charismatic people I've ever met. He had a presence that filled the room as soon as he entered it.

Chuck hired me for an after-school job. He asked questions and learned my story. I didn't know that God had given Chuck a call as well. His call was to mentor young men in the faith. This was a divine appointment.

For two years, I met Chuck in his office every week at 6:00 a.m. He put me through the paces of a rigorous spiritual course that included studying the Bible, memorizing verses, and keeping prayer lists. I learned spiritual disciplines I didn't expect, like time management, prioritizing tasks, and discerning the difference between the urgent and the important.

During my senior year, Chuck took me to Wendy's for lunch to share his plans to start a new business. He vaguely described the business, but he clearly wanted me to be a part of it. He asked if I would be willing to get an MBA and said he might be able to arrange for me to attend Harvard.

I shut him down. I was surprised he even brought it up. He knew my story; I had been called. I was going into ministry to serve and proclaim God's word. I had zero interest in business. I viewed it as boring, secular, and materialistic. Chuck told me to think about it, but it never came up again.

At the time, I had no idea that my early spiritual formation, learning to listen, submit, and change from the inside out, was quietly preparing me for a vocation I could never have imagined. It would take me years of wandering on paths I thought I was supposed to be on to find it.

I proceeded through school on my trajectory toward ministry. During my final semester, I discovered an opening for a youth pastor at a church back home. For those who don't know, youth ministry is often an entry-level position in a pastoral career. I applied, had a phone interview, and received a flush letter telling me I was not being considered for the job.

I got a surprise call from the chairman of the search committee a few months later. He said they'd been through several candidates, but they hadn't found the right fit. My name came back up, and the committee wanted to give me another interview. Then, they asked me to come for a weekend of in-person interviews and a congregational vote. As part of this final round of interviews, I would preach the sermon that Sunday morning right before the congregational vote. No pressure.

By the way, this was the same church where I had my dream-like vision seven years earlier. I stood on that same platform and preached, just like in my vision. I got the job.

I was in youth ministry for two years. I had great experiences and developed relationships that continue to this day. It was also a wake-up call. The church soon descended into a tumultuous season of transition. I quickly learned about angry, bitter people who will do anything to undermine you.

I learned that sometimes neither the pastor nor the board runs a church. Instead, rich, lifelong donors (who happen to employ some of the board members) call the shots in smoke-filled rooms behind closed doors. Hurt and disillusioned, I switched jobs. I signed a three-year contract to be the lead pastor of a rural Iowa church. I had an amazing experience, and I learned a lot. But it was also a season of hard life lessons. I felt like I didn't belong there, so I declined to renew my annual contract.

Another opportunity opened at a para-church men's ministry in the city. I thought maybe this was the ministry God had for me all along. I preached regularly to a room full of men, and I filled pulpits for vacationing pastors. And I didn't have to deal with the church politics that were the bane of my existence.

The challenge was that I had to raise half of my salary in support from friends and family. This is a very common practice in new ministries. Like the church jobs, this was an exciting position that gave me amazing opportunities and experiences. And again, initial enthusiasm quickly descended into unexpected hard lessons. When I was hired, I was told the ministry expected to pay my salary in the second year. However, as the end of my contract year drew near, my repeated requests to discuss my status were met with silence.

Ministry was proving to be painful. I couldn't stay with an organization whose leadership didn't care enough to discuss my livelihood. A week or two before my contract ended, I began calling my supporters and telling them not to send the next month's support check.

One of those supporters was my old spiritual mentor, Chuck Wenger.

"Why are you quitting?" he asked.

I told him.

"What are you going to do?"

I didn't know. I had nothing lined up, and I didn't know where to start. I hadn't even begun updating my resume.

"Have you announced your resignation? Are you sure you're going to quit?" he pressed.

"I don't know," I said hesitantly.

There was a pause at the other end of the phone.

"Make your decision within the hour and call me back," he said.

I called my wife. Then I prayed. Then I called Chuck back.

"I'm definitely quitting. I'm going to hand in my resignation this week," I told him.

"Meet me at the Village Inn on University at 2:00 this afternoon," he said abruptly.

A few hours later, we met and each ordered a soda. Chuck, in his typical charismatic style, told the server, "Don't worry. Small ticket. Big tip."

Chuck then looked at me.

"So, Tom. I have this business . . . ."

## "What Is It You Do?"

Of everyone, it was my mother who was most disappointed in my turn of career. I don't think she ever really understood it. As the years turned into decades, Mom asked two questions at least once every year. The first question was, "Are you ever returning to ministry?" The second question was,

"What is it you do?" We'll address both questions before we're finished, but I'd like to start with the second question.

"What is it you do?"

It's not only my mother who struggled with that question. Over the years we've had major clients who asked the same thing. It's an important question to answer before we go any further. In the early days of Intelligentics, Chuck made a big deal about everyone in the company knowing our mission statement. He incentivized us to memorize it. At our annual Christmas gathering, he gave "Wenger Bucks" to anyone who recited the mission statement from memory. The Wenger Bucks could then be used to purchase various tchotchkes and company logo wear.

Chuck also sent me to Disney University in Orlando to learn about the Disney way of customer service. I was there with about forty classmates. Many of them were from the C-suites of their companies. In fact, there was one major national restaurant chain that had its entire C-suite in attendance. Early in the week, the presenter asked if anyone knew their company's mission statement by heart. I raised my hand. I was the only one. I was asked to stand and recite it for everyone.

"c wenger group designs and implements customer-centered systems to measure and enhance service quality. By applying the principles of God's word to our lives and business, we become examples of servant leadership and integrity, bring measurable value to our clients, and profitably build our lives."

I guess the Wenger Bucks paid off in more ways than one.

### "c wenger group designs and implements customer-centered systems..."

To improve the customer experience, you must know your customers. Many leaders never make an effort to get to know their customers. They don't know who their customers are, what they think, or what drives their satisfaction. Helping them find out is at the heart of what we do.

Many clients do a comprehensive Voice of the Customer (VOC) survey every two to three years. During a VOC survey, customers evaluate every touchpoint with the company, from marketing to ordering and returns. These regular surveys provide the leaders with the data to understand what will enhance or hinder customer satisfaction. It provides the CEO with a blueprint for leading the vision and holding their team accountable. I always liken this to a biannual physical, a company health check from their customers.

Most companies I know skip the annual physical. Instead, they wait until acute symptoms appear. Many of our clients come to us with burning questions or ailments.

"We're not attracting Millennials or Gen Z customers. Why?"

"We just went through a merger. How do we understand customers to create a successful blended family?"

"Technology is changing how we do business. What do our customers think and need?"

We then gather both quantitative and qualitative data to figure out what their customers think. It's then that the prescription for what's ailing them becomes clear.

Our team knows how to talk to customers, ask the right questions, and get inside their heads. Admittedly, similar market and customer research firms are common. Some clients come to us simply for research. But for some clients, research is the first step toward transforming the customer experience. Their destination is a corporate culture of service excellence and continuous improvement.

Let me use our company's mission statement to walk you through what it is we do.

## *"...customer-centered systems to measure and enhance service quality..."*

We were approached by one of our clients' executives, who were suffering from acute sleep loss. Amazon Business announced it was entering their market. My client was terrified of the impact.

They had never done any kind of customer survey. Intelligentics designed a strategic positioning analysis to discover what customers in their space thought about both my client and their purchase intent with Amazon Business and similar competitors.

I entered the boardroom like a physician entering an exam room with the results of the MRI. I had some good news and some bad news.

The good news was that Amazon Business wasn't yet a threat in their market. The executives could get a good night's sleep. The bad news was that our client's customer satisfaction was mediocre at best.

As I shared this information, I couldn't help noticing the giant sign on the wall proclaiming the company's commitment to the customer. A board member pointed to the sign and told the CEO, "We're not doing that."

Quality assessment (QA) done well is a rigorous investigation of the interactions between a company and its customers. It's most common to hear "This call may be monitored," but the process works for phone, email, chat, and text.

I discovered fascinating results when I reviewed the results of the customer research. Customers who placed an order via email were less satisfied than those who did so by phone. When I shared the results with the CEO, he asked, "What's wrong with our email?"

That's the right question, and it's what makes what we do at Intelligentics different from most market research firms. I told the CEO we could identify the issue with a random sample of 100 emails over a four-week period. He was wise to let us do a Service Quality Assessment™ (SQA) of their team's email communication. Strategic positioning research gave us a great demographic picture of the client's customers. In this case, the typical customer was a male engineer in his fifties or sixties.

Yet most of the sales and support team were young Millennials. Our SQA revealed that emails were being treated like text messages. There were one-line replies to complex emails without punctuation or formatting and they were full of acronyms. It was no wonder that satisfaction with email communication was so low.

So now our client knew that their customers were less than satisfied. They knew the source and what their team was doing that was driving that dissatisfaction. There was a gap between the customer's expectations and the experience the team provided every day in countless email exchanges.

It was time to fill the gap.

We presented a data-informed custom training for our client's sales and support teams. We showed them what their customers said about their email communication. We then trained them on the standard elements and structure of a professionally formatted and written email.

In less than a year, customer satisfaction with our client's email communication rose almost 20 percentage points. They could now point to the sign on the boardroom wall and confirm that they were making good on their promise to provide a good customer experience. They had the data to prove it.

It's so simple, it's almost profound.

Do you know what your customers expect and whether they are satisfied with your service?

We do the research to find out.

Do you know what your customers experience when they interact with your team in the daily moments of truth?

Our SQA provides you with that data from the customer's point of view.

Do you know how to efficiently and effectively move the needle on improving the customer experience?

It's not hard if you know what your customers expect, what your team is delivering, and where the gap lies. It's simply a matter of targeted coaching and training to fill the holes.

When consistently employed together, these three steps become a cycle of continuous improvement.

## Integrated Model for Continuous Improvement

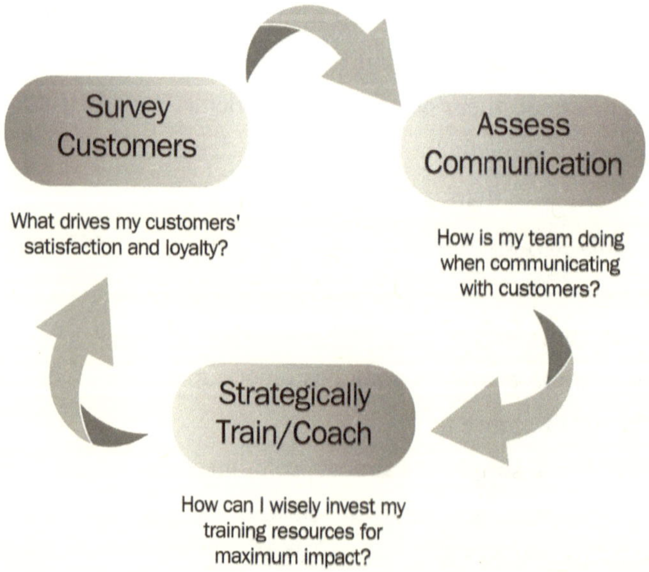

Customer-centered systems measure and enhance service quality and the customer experience. We have served some of our clients for over twenty-five years with this methodology, a simple cycle of continuous improvement.

**"...by applying the principles of God's Word to our lives and work, we become examples of servant leadership and integrity..."**

I had entered business, a world I had wanted nothing to do with. I didn't understand it. I had never wanted to. But I prayed a prayer of surrender when I was fourteen years old. Whatever God wanted. Wherever He led.

Jesus led me to this business, but this wasn't just any business. This was a company founded by my spiritual mentor. When I was a young man, Chuck mentored me in the way of Jesus. Now, he was going to mentor me in the ways of business.

Up to this point, I had considered the two to be exclu sive. They were separate worlds. Under Chuck's guidance, I quickly discovered that I couldn't have been more wrong. Chuck taught me that foundational business and customer service come right from the Bible. Let me give you a few simple examples.

## Treat Customers the Way You Want to Be Treated

Countless times clients have quoted the Golden Rule to me during discussions about their customer service.

Many of those clients have no idea that the source of the quote is Jesus.

> **So in everything, do to others what you would have them do to you, for this sums up the Law and the Prophets.**
> **Matthew 7:12**

When I began working with clients, I was surprised by people I met who not only quoted the principle but also knew the source. Senior vice presidents and CSRs showed me how it applied in both business and life.

My first client was a major national retailer with contact centers around the country. They had hundreds of CSRs answering calls 24/7/365. In my first days on the job, I noticed a CSR who stood out. He had the longest hair I'd ever seen on a man. His hair hung all the way down to his butt. He seemed to be a great guy. He was always smiling. There was just something about him.

Eventually, I learned that the young man was a Christian. He had long hair because he'd taken a Nazarite vow. This is an ancient, biblical, Hebrew practice in which one refrains from cutting their hair for a prescribed time period. This young man had a friend whose tragic life mistake landed him in prison. He vowed to pray for his friend every day and leave his hair uncut until his friend was released. In this way, his friend would know he was loved and not forgotten. I have never seen such a commitment to a friend.

Here I was in what many referred to as a sweatshop contact center, witnessing a spiritual example I'd never witnessed inside a church.

What do you think I found when I assessed the same CSR's phone calls? This young man was exemplary. He treated customers with servant-hearted enthusiasm. He genuinely and sincerely applied the Golden Rule in everything he did in life, including serving customers on the phone. I didn't have much to teach him. He had a lot to teach me both about being a follower of Jesus and about giving a great customer experience.

## Go the Extra Mile

Jesus lived in Israel when it was part of the Roman Empire. Throughout his entire life, Jesus knew the Romans as enemies and occupiers of His homeland. By law, a Roman soldier could conscript any person he chose to carry his gear for one mile. Everyone was familiar with the law because Roman soldiers took full advantage of it. Jesus's followers and fellow citizens had all been forced to walk behind a Roman soldier schlepping his heavy rucksack. Therefore, it was a bit of a shock when Jesus told them to offer an additional mile.

The guiding principle behind Jesus's teaching was to surprise people by doing the unexpected. Everyone walked the mile. Refusal was punishable by death. But no one would willingly walk an additional mile. To do so would have shocked not only the Roman soldier but also Jesus's fellow Jewish citizens under occupation. The shock sparked attention and created buzz. It also led to other conversations.

I start large group client trainings by asking for personal stories about great customer service they've experienced. One company is mentioned drastically more than any other. The company is Chick-fil-A.

I commonly hear stories of Chick-fil-A managers in the parking lot on a rainy day escorting people to the building under a big umbrella. Others talk about having the door opened and being personally greeted. The list goes on. Chick-fil-A customers are shocked when they experience what other fast-food restaurants would never do. That's the extra-mile principle at work.

Jesus's extra-mile lesson is even more powerful knowing that his audience had to make the effort for their oppressors. Many front-line CSRs slide into viewing customers as oppressors. The CSR is paid to respond to them, but customers can be ignorant, misguided, rude, and unreasonable. The extra mile takes Jesus-style faith and chutzpah if you have a customers-are-idiots attitude.

## If You Want to Be Great, You Must Be the Servant of All

When Jesus uttered this principle, He wasn't speaking to the crowds like the previous two principles I mentioned. He spoke these words to his own team at Jesus, Inc. His twelve direct reports were arguing over who would get the corner office of the C-suite and the top box on the org chart.

Jesus even provided a memorable example on the eve of His execution. On His last day as earthly CEO, Jesus did what was expected of the lowest employee on the org chart. It was an act so menial that typically only immigrants hired by a third-party vendor did such a thing. Jesus washed the dirty, dusty feet of His direct reports.

Contact center front-line supervisors have one of the most difficult jobs in the organization. And I've observed the one thing that great leaders in this position do consistently to make a difference. They are happy to oblige when a CSR asks, "Will you talk to this customer for me? I'm at my wits' end."

I've observed the difference in team member respect between supervisors who step up and those who refuse. CSRs feel the dismissal loud and clear when their boss says: "I don't talk to customers. That's your job."

The principle applies at every level of the organization. I knew a senior executive in charge of a large, notoriously broken customer service operation. He had just been tasked with turning that aircraft carrier around in the rough seas of the company's corporate culture.

He began by sitting through training for front-line CSRs. After training, he sported the company-issue headset, sat in the contact center, and took customer phone calls like everybody else. He learned what was working and what was broken, and he shocked every team member on the org chart.

His entire team were like Roman soldiers asking, "I'm sorry. What did you say? You want to walk another mile?" He created the buzz necessary for an operation cynically entrenched in dysfunction to think, "This guy is different. Perhaps this whole thing can change." He earned the respect of everyone on the team at every level. He created the crucial conversations that had to take place to turn things around.

That executive was also a faithful follower of Jesus.

## Bless Those Who Curse You

Jesus said that everyone loves those who love them. Doing the unexpected is what makes a difference, just like carrying the Roman's rucksack an extra mile or the CEO taking customer calls. No one does that.

Are you sensing a theme?

Customer support can be a rough job. Angry customers curse their fellow human beings, forgetting there's a real person on the other end of the line. They think they are talking to a company. It's easy to dismiss a disembodied voice. By its very nature, the interaction feels impersonal, and that is fertile soil for unhealthy emotions.

Across my career, I've witnessed countless CSRs who learned the art of turning that situation around. They bless an angry customer by responding with empathy, personal interaction, and advocacy. The voice who began crying out with anger ends the call exclaiming "You just made my day."

## Doing with Attitude Is Better Than Refusing with Lip Service

Jesus spoke in parables—short stories with a simple moral. One of his parables was about two sons whose ol' man told them to do a chore. One son said, "Sure," but then he blew it off. The other son said, "No way," but then he actually did it. The moral of the story is that it's not what you say but what you do that counts.

When I work with front-line agents, my feedback is not always met with enthusiasm. Quite the opposite.

One of my first coaching gigs was with a team selling components used in everything from microwaves to the International Space Station. One inside sales representative was a brash young man full of swagger and bravado. I was seated at a table in the conference room when we entered our first coaching session. He strode right next to me, hovered over me, and let me have it with both barrels.

"I want you to [expletive] know that you don't know a [expletive] thing about my job. There is nothing you can [expletive] teach me that's going to make a [expletive] difference in what I do."

We were off to a great start.

I coached that salesman quarterly for over twenty years. I watched him rise from inside sales to an exclusive role as a global sales account manager. He never had a great attitude when I coached him. He treated me with derision for a long time. But my analysis and the resulting data revealed that he also slowly began to incorporate the tactics I taught him and his team. He would never admit it, but he did what I suggested. It made him a better salesman.

One of the greatest compliments I've ever received in my career was twenty years later when he addressed new inside sales reps in a team meeting. He told them, "You're gonna hate the quarterly meeting with Tom. You'll hate listening to your calls, but it's important. It makes a difference."

### *"...bring measurable value to our clients, and profitably build our lives."*

My job is about more than listening to phone call after phone call after phone call. It's about making a tangible difference for our client. To that requires me to pay attention to a number of individuals: the customer, the agent, the front-line manager, and the CEO.

Bringing measurable value to our clients and their customers requires making a difference in people's daily lives. The data from our research and QA has to be applied. That means teaching clients different ways of doing what they do every day. It means motivating them, inspiring them, equipping them, holding them accountable, and telling them things they don't want to hear.

I was shocked to discover how much I loved my job. The call analysis itself can be mind-numbingly tedious, but the reward of working with people at every level of a business is amazing. Serving people with knowledge and helping them succeed in their jobs and their lives has been more fulfilling than I could have imagined.

Many clients have told me that our time together not only helped them succeed at business, it also made them better people. That is what has made the tedium of analyzing 100,000 phone calls worth it.

I love my clients. I've had a chance to walk with people, not only on their vocational journeys but in their life journeys. The names and faces are flooding back to me even as I write these words. The dear woman I was scheduled to coach right after she got a diagnosis of terminal cancer. The rough-and-tumble career salesman who broke down like a baby because he suddenly realized that he'd hit the glass ceiling. The front-line manager who came to the realization that she was powerless over alcohol. The CEO who confessed that the corner office felt like solitary confinement. I love each of these individuals. I've been honored to be a part of their careers and their lives.

Faith is at the center of our company's mission statement. However, we've never been particularly overt about it except through our active endeavor to exemplify it in everything we do. I'm quite convinced that most of my clients over the years have never read our mission statement. They have no idea how much faith plays in our lives and work.

Our job is to bring measurable value, and we do. The data shows that our clients' customer satisfaction is improving. Our clients keep coming back year after year, some for well over twenty years.

The fact that I endeavored to be part of vocational ministry and ended up with a career in business landed me in an interesting place. I found myself a part of both worlds at the same time.

I never stopped preaching. Regardless of what church my family and I found ourselves attending, I was asked to preach and teach. We've attended the same church for two decades. I'm scheduled to preach regularly, even though I'm not a staff member. I've even had the privilege of coaching and mentoring young staff members in the art and craft of preaching. But it's not my career or my vocation.

I spend my life in two very different worlds. Members of each of those worlds don't know what to make of me when they discover that I'm part of the other. Sometimes business executives treat me with a bit of suspicion because they don't understand my spiritual passion. I've even been blackballed by clients because of it. Likewise, I've experienced church staff holding me at arm's length and regarding me with suspicion. It feels like I'm not committed because ministry is not my full-time vocation.

What I've discovered is that the worlds of business and ministry are more alike than either would care to admit. Through my spiritual journey, I have learned invaluable lessons I've passed on to clients to help them succeed. I've learned things in my business career that have helped me spiritually succeed in life and relationships.

This book is about lessons from assessing thousands of phone calls and leveraging the results to help clients improve customer experience. It's also about spiritual lessons my career has taught me along the way. Throughout the book I include breakout "Life Lesson" sections with lessons from my career that have applied to my spiritual life.

## Life Lesson: The Job Matters to God

*Whatever you do, do it all for the glory of God.*
1 Corinthians 10:31

*You are the light of the world. A town built*
*on a hill cannot be hidden.*
Matthew 5:14

*But you are a chosen people, a royal priesthood.*
1 Peter 2:9

Before the Reformation in 1517, the institutional church was a rigid spiritual caste system. Priests were the elite upper class. They had all the power and wealth spiritually, socially, and often physically. The Reformation changed all that. Martin Luther, John Calvin, and Ulrich Zwingli all stressed that the Bible refers to all believers as being God's "royal priesthood." They likewise stressed that God uses every believer in every vocation. Luther exalted the milkmaid's milking, the cobbler's stitching, and the mother's diaper-changing as sacred acts when done in faith. Vocation was ministry, not second-class labor.

However, humans inevitably return to their defaults. It's generally assumed that ministry is a professional vocation carried out by a pastor, and business is for common people. It's what I believed sitting with Chuck at that Wendy's years ago. The Bible clearly teaches there is no difference, but our practical reality indicates that most people don't believe it.

Jesus taught that God's kingdom on earth begins with every individual being the light of Christ everywhere they go and in everything they do. This includes work. Paul used the metaphor of being the "fragrance" of Christ everywhere he went. He also observed the fragrance was a pleasing aroma that caused some people to stop for another whiff. Others recoiled as if it were the stench of death. I experience the same thing every time I enter a client's office.

The way I run my business and how I interact with others says something about what I truly believe. It also has an impact on others as I endeavor to serve them well and go the extra mile.

For years I poured myself into learning about faith, integrity, and human behavior. Little did I know it would resurface in an unlikely place: the recorded conversations between customers and the people paid to serve them.

# CHAPTER 2

# Foundations of Quality Assessment (QA)

The systematic assessment of customer interactions and resulting data can help any business build customer satisfaction, sales, retention, and loyalty. Throughout my career, I learned foundational principles I share with every new client. Then I need to remind the client of these principles repeatedly.

Intelligentics is unique because we go beyond assessment and data reporting. We provide actionable insight, and we help clients make tactical improvements. Every organization is just as unique as the people who make it successful, but there are a few timeless foundational principles. In this chapter, we'll talk about the foundations of quality assessment.

## Customer Service Rule #1: Do the Best You Can with What You Have

I was assessing calls for a company that provides a certain type of in-home services. A customer called to schedule an appointment. The CSR was pleasant and courteous but explained to the customer that the town where she lived was in her colleague's territory. Her colleague was at lunch, and she didn't have access to the information. The customer was going to have to wait for a call back.

This is a simple example of single-point failure. A customer is calling. They want to do business with you. They are ready to make an appointment and utilize your services. Instead, they have to wait, and any number of things could happen in between. The CSR could miss the message after lunch and never call the customer back. The customer could decide that they don't have time to wait and call a competitor. An agonizing game of phone tag could commence that ends in both parties giving up on reaching one another.

Should the CSR I'm assessing be held responsible and accountable for not resolving the customer's request? Certainly not. She did her job. Management created a process set up as a single-point failure.

A common frustration among front-line agents is a broken system, partial information, or wrong information. QA is powerful and profitable because it quickly finds systemic pain points that impede a great customer experience. In my experience, businesses rarely listen to the agents who know the pain points best. And the more corporate layers there are between the CSR's cubicle and the CEO's office, the less likely it is that anything will change.

Thus, my never-ending mantra to every front-line agent is Customer Service Rule #1: Do the best you can with what you have. You won't always have the information you need. Technology will not always work for you the way it was promised. There are always going to be times when management tells you one thing and reality is completely different.

I've asked countless reps, "Did you do the best you could for this customer despite not having the resources to help them?"

When the agent affirms that they did, I reply, "Then pat yourself on the back. Sleep well tonight. Find contentment in knowing that you did the best you could with what you had."

**Contentment isn't passive. It's an active choice to rest in what you've done while continuing to strive for better. That same mindset applies to service excellence.**

The journey to consistent service excellence is not a sprint. It's a marathon. Service excellence requires more than great front-line agents. It requires all systems and teams working together for an optimal customer experience. That doesn't happen overnight. In the meantime, team members at every level of the operation have to embrace Customer

Service Rule #1. We're not where we want to be. We are, however, making progress. In the moment, I have to find contentment.

## Life Lesson: Contentment

Along my life journey, I've come to realize that Customer Service Rule #1 applies to life as much as it does to business. There is so much about life and our circumstances that we don't control. Life has thrown me many curveballs.

- My good friend being hit by a drunk driver and left brain dead

- A friend who slid into depression and became suicidal

- My father's diagnosis with multiple myeloma

- My mother's diagnoses of both autoimmune hepatitis and Alzheimer's

- My wife's and my years-long struggle through infertility

Like a CSR who never knows what the next call will bring, we don't know what life will throw at us. Paul of Tarsus knew a thing or two about that. Paul spent his adult life traveling through the Roman Empire, sharing Jesus's message with others. Paul described his struggles to the believers in the city of Corinth.

> *I have worked much harder, been in prison more frequently, been flogged more severely, and been exposed to death again and again. Five times I received from the Jews the forty lashes minus one. Three times I was beaten with rods, once I was pelted with stones, three times I was shipwrecked, I spent a night and a day in the open sea, I have been constantly on the move. I have been in danger from rivers, in danger from bandits, in danger from my fellow Jews, in danger from Gentiles; in danger in the city, in danger in the country, in danger at sea; and in danger from false believers. I have labored and toiled and have often gone without sleep; I have known hunger and thirst and have often gone without food; I have been cold and naked. Besides everything else, I face daily the pressure of my concern for all the churches.*
> 2 Corinthians 11:23b–28

I'm not sure I would have made it if I had experienced everything Paul went through. So, it is even more mind-blowing to read his words to the believers in Philippi.

> *I am not saying this because I am in need, for I have learned to be content whatever the circumstances. I know what it is to be in need, and I know what it is to have plenty. I have*

> *learned the secret of being content in any and every situation, whether well fed or hungry, whether living in plenty or in want. I can do all this through Him who gives me strength.*
> Philippians 4:11–13

I worked at multiple locations of a Christian bookstore chain during high school and college. I sold countless frisbees, t-shirts, key chains, and bookmarks with Paul's words "I can do all things through Christ who strengthens me" printed on them. Standing alone, it's easy to think he's talking about accomplishing Marvel action hero-type feats of superhuman proportion. But that's not what he's talking about. When he wrote, "I can do all things through Christ," he was talking about being content in suffering.

Paul learned how to do the best he could in life with what he had every day. Every day, I'm striving to do the same, no matter my circumstances. But these lessons weren't confined to church pews or family kitchens. They showed up vividly and repeatedly in the data, the calls, and the patterns of business I began to see through quality assessment.

## Rules and Exceptions

Early in my career, I was in Tennessee to provide customer service training. Our client was a national retailer with contact centers across the country operating 24/7/365. My training session was an hour long, and there were hundreds of CSRs working in three shifts around the clock. The client pulled CSRs off the phone ten or twenty at a time. I trained every day, at all hours, for an entire week. It was a gauntlet.

Amidst the gauntlet, I noticed a pattern in the responses from the CSRs when I discussed how using the customer's name personalizes the conversation and meets the desire for a personal service relationship.

A hand would go up in the air.

"Yeah, but Tom . . . ." (It always began with *Yeah, but*.)

"This one time . . . ." (It was always *this one time*)

"Yeah, but Tom? This one time I mistakenly called them by the wrong name. They got really offended and started yelling at me. So, I decided I am never making that mistake again. I never use the customer's name."

It didn't matter what customer service skill I was teaching. There was always a "Yeah, but."

Think, however, about what the CSRs were saying. In their daily full-time shift, they might take around 100 phone calls. That's 500 calls a week and 2,000 calls a month. You have 2,000 opportunities to provide a personable, friendly, and empathetic customer experience. But because one customer reacted negatively, you've decided that all 2,000 will get a diminished service experience.

The CSRs made general rules about call handling based on exceptional situations. They ensured that all of their customers received a mediocre experience as the general rule. The client had a reputation for poor to mediocre service. Agents making rules from exceptions was part of the systemic problem the client needed to address. Brand reputations are made from customers' general rule experiences.

Think about any fast-food chain. My brother has a sign business, and for several years his only client has been a fast-food chain. He travels the country painting the same murals and signs on new stores the chain opens. He's ensuring that customers have a visually positive experience every time they walk in at any location.

Fast-food chains go to great lengths to ensure that you have a general rule type of experience. The buildings look the same. The menu is the same. The uniforms are the same. The experience is the generally same. They understand the value customers place on being able to depend on an interaction that's consistent and dependable.

The same thing is true for any and every business and customer. Every point of contact is an opportunity to win or lose a customer. You want to make the most of every customer interaction. That doesn't happen naturally. Trust me. I have both the experience and the data to prove it.

When a team does a first-time SQA, the results are typically a bell curve. A few reps are at the extremes, naturally providing either consistently good or consistently poor customer experiences. Most reps reside between the two giving inconsistent and mediocre customer experiences. The result? Depending on which agent picks up the phone, the customer could have a very different experience. That inconsistency undermines customer satisfaction, loyalty, and retention, and with it, the bottom line.

Most business leaders don't appreciate this reality. They are unwilling to invest in an excellent customer experience through every channel. Technology is relatively easy to fix. Human beings are messier and more difficult to work with. But it can be done, it can be done well, and it can measurably improve customer sales, satisfaction, retention, and loyalty.

Intelligentics has been doing it for almost forty years.

## Life Lesson: Rules and Exceptions in Our World and Everyday Lives

As I began to contemplate rules and exceptions, I started to see the principle at work everywhere. Take news, for example.

My first job was delivering the *Des Moines Tribune* every weekday to subscribers in a four-block section of my neighborhood. Then, I would return home and proceed to read the newspaper I had just delivered.

In the old days of newsprint, editors had to fill any open spaces at the end of an article. They would find an interesting, sensational tidbit and condense it into the three or four lines called a "blurb." I was always fascinated by blurbs. A dam breaking in some region of China killed over a thousand people. An earthquake in Afghanistan leveled an entire city. A massive flood in Bengal left thousands homeless. It was sensational but remote and distant. It didn't have the impact of the local and national news that dominated the rest of the newspaper. Blurbs were exceptional; the local and national news was the general rule.

Now we live in a 24/7/365 news cycle where news outlets are desperate for views and clicks. News is business, after all. Views and clicks drive advertising revenue. What gets people to view and click? General news is easy to pass over; what's sensational stops the scroll. And so, what used to be a blurb at the bottom of page sixteen dominates a news cycle if people engage.

Being mindful of rules and exceptions has also helped me be a wise consumer of news. A few years ago, specialists in Tourette's Syndrome reported a sudden and unexplainable surge in cases. As I read, I immediately thought there was something that didn't add up. Tourette's is uncommon. Less than one percent of the population is diagnosed with it. It's an exception. The news was telling me that it was suddenly becoming more of a general rule affliction of adolescent females world-wide. My internal alarm bells went off.

As the story unfolded, it was discovered that the common denominator was social media. In particular, TikTok. Girls with diagnosed Tourette's garnered millions of views and likes by putting their symptoms on display. Suddenly, adolescent girls decided that they had Tourette's symptoms to display on TikTok, too. Their desire for popularity caused them to adopt an exceptional condition as their general-rule reality.

I even see exceptions and rules sneaking into daily life at home. A rare relational mistake is translated into a general rule reason for constant mistrust. A teenager observes the broad boundaries set by one friend's libertine parent and then reports that as a general rule everybody has such freedom. They are the exceptionally maligned teenager on the entire social landscape.

I also realized that rules and exceptions can be leveraged for positive effect. Years ago, my wife and I decided to apply the principle to our daily routine. As a general rule, what things do we use and depend on every day for our quality of life? A decent night's sleep makes a huge difference in how we feel and function every day. So we invested in a good mattress and a bedroom environment conducive to a good night's sleep. Likewise, a great cup of coffee is something the two of us value every morning to start our day off right. We purchased a nice grind-and-brew coffee maker. It saves us money in the long run. We spend very little on expensive coffee from local coffee shops. It also ensures a positive start to every single day.

On the other hand, I'm not the world's best handyman. Renovation, remodel, and repair are neither my interests nor my strengths. As a general rule, I avoid anything more than light and simple home repairs. So why would I invest in a garage full of expensive, top-of-the-line power tools?

Investment in a high-end mattress makes sense. I need a good night's sleep every day as a general rule. Investment in a garage full of high-end tools is foolish. I only need a few basic tools for occasional easy home maintenance tasks.

The rules and exceptions principle even finds itself in the Great Story God authors between Genesis and Revelation. In Numbers 33, God told Moses to record a comprehensive list of all the stages of the Hebrews' journey. It's a long chronological list of places the Hebrews camped for 38 years. Nothing happens for the entire chapter. Many people fall off the wagon on their New Year's resolution to read through the entire Bible when they reach Numbers 33.

So why would God tell Moses to save this list for posterity?

Let's hold that question for a moment as we consider the next foundational principle of QA.

## Most Interactions Are Boring and Mundane

"100,000 phone calls? Oh my! I bet you've heard some really interesting things!"

I have heard some interesting things. One of my colleagues once suggested that we keep an archive of legendary calls. Then, when an analyst reaches a certain point of seniority in the company, they get to listen to all of them as a reward.

That's a great idea, but there are two problems. One is security. For the sake of confidentiality, we always destroy the recordings. The second reason is that there just wouldn't be that many of them. Business calls and emails are transactional by nature. They are mind-numbingly routine. The slog of everyday business. So much so that the grind of analyzing calls gets to be too much for some QA analysts.

Our team once did a pilot assessment for the scheduling department of a large regional healthcare provider. I was in a leadership position at that time, but I wasn't yet managing our SQA team. I worked on the project, but a colleague was responsible for a majority of the call analysis and the report.

My colleague was young, single, and full of life and adventure. He also happened to be in love in a long-distance relationship. He was distracted, to say the least. He decided he couldn't handle listening to and analyzing hundreds of mundane, routine scheduling phone calls.

So he made it all up. The data and the call summaries in the report were fabricated.

In retrospect, I'm happy that the client caught it. It was a particularly painful and costly event in my career and in the history of Intelligentics. Another colleague and I redid the entire project for free, including a refund of all previous payments. Trust was broken. We lost the client and the opportunity for a profitable long-term relationship. Those conversations and client meetings were among the most difficult things I've had to do in my career. It was all because one analyst couldn't handle analyzing so many tedious customer interactions. They were so routine and dull that they pushed an honest, decent person to risk their career.

Business interactions between companies and customers are routine and boring. This reality poses both a threat and an opportunity for any business leader.

The threat is the temptation to ignore such everyday interactions. It's easy to think that if they are so routine and tedious, there must be nothing of value in analyzing them. This mindset is especially alluring for larger operations because the task feels overwhelming. There are just too many silos, too many teams, and too many interactions. So, executives just don't think about it. Put it out of your head. After all, it's just routine; what could go wrong? What could I possibly gain from assessing mundane, routine customer interactions?

Actually, a lot can go wrong in the course of thousands of routine interactions. Customers don't get answers or resolutions. They get caught in systemic loops with no way out. A few customers have a good experience while callers who get the CSR on the opposite end of the bell curve take their business elsewhere. Then there are the majority of customers whose experiences are mediocre at best. They may or may not return, depending on which of your competitors offers a sale next month.

The opportunity is discovering all the ways to consistently improve your customers' experience with every interaction. These opportunities are sitting there just waiting to be mined. There are so ways to turn a routine interaction into a positive experience your customer doesn't expect. There are so many ways to transform costly problems into win-win scenarios for you and your customers.

After analyzing over 100,000 phone calls, I can tell you definitively that there is profitable value in measuring the mundane. I believe even God would agree.

## Life Lesson: The Importance of the Mundane

Let's return to the question about Numbers 33. Why would God ask Moses and the Hebrews to keep this long chronological list of places they camped in the wilderness for thirty-eight years?

Most of us have seen the film *The Ten Commandments* or the animated equivalent, *Prince of Egypt*. It's the story of the ancient Hebrew tribes' momentous deliverance from slavery as recorded in the Book of Exodus. Forty years later, the Book of Joshua describes how the Hebrew tribes crossed into the Promised Land.

What took place during the forty years between these historical events? It was mundane, general rule, walking through the wilderness day after day. God was faithful to the Hebrews the entire time. He protected, He provided, He blessed, and He was present in both the exceptional events and the long, boring, general rule slog.

To this day, Jews use Numbers 33 as liturgy. They chant the endless list of encampments as a reminder that God is present in the mundane slog. He has a purpose in the ordinary.

In her book *Liturgy of the Ordinary*, Tish Harrison Warren wrote about the spiritual nature of daily life. There is a spiritual cadence, a purpose in making the bed, pouring morning coffee, and packing the kids' lunches. God is present in the routine machinations of each typical day.

Life and business are filled with both exceptional moments and general rule, mundane slog. As a follower of Jesus, I've learned the importance of recognizing God's presence and purpose in both. It's important to instill the mundane with purpose and excellence. You never know when something exceptionally marvelous will emerge.

## Every Interaction Is an Opportunity

Let's return for a moment to Gen Z and fast-food restaurants. Research reveals that Gen Z chooses not to answer the phone. They find anxiety in the unknown and the unexpected. They need to feel safe and confident about who is calling and what the call's about. Similarly, fast-food restaurants focus on a consistent customer experience no matter which location you visit.

Consumers don't want to do business with a company that channels Forrest Gump's proverbial box of chocolates. They want to know what they're going to get from you. Today I may talk to the CSR on the positive end of the bell curve but tomorrow could be the opposite. That makes me hesitant to call. It makes me hesitant even to want to do business with you. I've heard countless calls in which customers asked a great CSR, "How can I contact you directly every time I call?"

A consistent, pleasant customer experience drives loyalty and retention.

Every call, email, chat session, and text message is an opportunity to build customer loyalty. The key is to create a consistent, pleasant experience that your customers can count on every time.

The foundational first step of QA is to define what you want the customer to experience to look like from the greeting to the closing. Here's a typical flow.

1. Greet the customer.
2. Determine the issue.
3. Pull up the account.
4. Verify the caller.
5. Answer the question(s).
6. Ensure that all questions/issues have been resolved.
7. Close the call.

Next, we define what we want our customers to experience in each step of the interaction.

After the preferred experience and the elements of that experience are defined, the team must be trained. They must know what is expected of them and how they will be held accountable. Expectations should be communicated when a new agent is onboarded. Team members should be held accountable for these expectations throughout their careers. Every customer interaction should be a standard of your brand, just like the silhouette of a building identifies a fast-food chain. Be sure not to settle for a good interaction. Your competitors are good. You want to make it great. When it comes to making things great, I've learned from both scripture and the stage.

# Life Lesson: The Difference Between Good and Great

As I've progressed in my spiritual journey, I have spent more time and meditation on the Old Testament. What I once found boring and meaningless is now filled with connection and depth that has taken my spiritual life to a new level. The key is reading and thinking about the text from a different perspective. Preachers, teachers, and commentators tend to zoom in on individual words, verses, and sections. I step back and look at what God is doing with a wide-angle lens. It makes all the difference.

For example, many readers skim God's detailed instructions for the design and construction of His Tabernacle in Exodus 31–40. Step back and consider what God is doing in wide-angle context.

- The Creator of the universe is planning to dwell on earth among the Hebrew tribes.

- Every measurement, every material, every stitch shouts that God is holy. He isn't casual about worship. The thoroughness shows that approaching God requires reverence, structure, and care.

- Acacia wood overlaid with gold and fine linen in blue, purple, and scarlet with cherubim woven in. Even the artistry itself was an offering. Beauty matters to God. Craftsmanship is spiritual service.

- Men and women brought freewill offerings. Artisans, craftsmen, and weavers poured their skills into the project. The Tabernacle was not Moses's project; it was a people's collective act of devotion. Worship is richer when everyone contributes.

- The Tabernacle is seen as a foreshadowing of Christ. He is the true High Priest, the Lamb on the altar, the Bread on the table, the Light of the world, and ultimately the Tabernacle Himself, God dwelling among us.

- Just as the Hebrews were called to exactness in building God's dwelling, we are called to be attentive in building lives of faith. The Spirit works both in the grand design and in the tiniest stitch of obedience.

All the boring, repetitive details offer spiritual insight. God cares about details, and if I want to be like Him, I should, too.

I've been blogging my chapter-a-day devotional thoughts every weekday on tomvanderwell.com since 2006. I've written thousands of devotional blog posts.

I've blogged through the entire Bible multiple times. The content has been and always will be free. You're welcome to subscribe at tomvanderwell.com.

In all my years of blogging, I've had only one blog post go viral. It wasn't even a devotional post.

My one viral post was a momentary brainstorm I had on a plane flying home from a business trip. I tapped it out in ten minutes and posted it when I got home. The title is "Ten Ways Being a Theater Major Prepared Me for Success." It was February 2012, and the post had over 100,000 views that month alone. I started getting comments and emails from Hollywood producers and Broadway actors and actresses. To this day, it still gets a ton of views every month. The post speaks to something true that no voice had really trumpeted.

My theater training prepared me for my career in ways I could never have imagined. It gave me a thorough understanding of effective human communication in all forms. It taught me practical project management. It taught me how to improvise in the moment. It taught me how to empathize, understand, and care about diverse sets of characters, both heroes and villains.

Chuck wanted me to get a business degree. Looking back, I'm pretty sure God knew my degree in theater would serve me better in the job He had for me to do.

I had a great theater professor. He was so good, in fact, that while I was in school, he created what would become a wildly successful television show. Within a few years, he moved to Hollywood and became a producer and director.

My professor had a mantra that he drilled into me: "The difference between good and great is in the details."

For over a decade, I served as the president of our local, small-town community theater. I have also had the honor of working on film projects with celebrated directors and Hollywood actors. In fact, in the old parlor game Six Degrees of Kevin Bacon, you can get from me to Kevin Bacon in just three degrees. The craft of staging a show on stage may be the same in community theater and professional productions, but there is a world of difference between the two.

The difference is in the details.

In theater, the details include disciplines such as character development and exploration, beating the script, playing with subtext, and experimenting with line deliveries. The details require an investment of time and energy, but the rewards are apparent on the stage. Audiences sense the difference between actors who just follow the script and those who transform into a different character.

Most business owners and executives run their companies the way a community theater produces a musical. You're on the business stage. You've memorized your sales pitch. You go through the basic blocking of business. Sell, deliver, repeat.

The show goes on. Money is made. But it could be so much better. You could grow your audience and pack the house. Your customers could be far more satisfied. You could leave them dying to return and bring their friends. But that requires more than going through the basics. It requires paying attention to details like an engaged actor or the God who refuses to live in any old tent from Camping World.

The difference between good and great is in the details. In business, this means paying attention to and transforming the regular interactions your front line has with your customers. This includes interactions with sales, service, support, accounting, collections, and even your receptionists. After all, Dale Carnegie taught us all that you never get a second chance to make a first impression.

Every business day is a performance by your team. Every time an associate picks up the phone and every time they reply to an email, the curtain rises for a customer. It's showtime, and the customer is your captive audience. Are you going to be good enough for them not to walk out, or are you going to be so great that they come back for more with their friends and loved ones in tow? This is the front line of business.

# The Front Line of Business

When it comes to understanding the importance of service excellence on the front lines of business, it's easy to understand the importance for the theme parks, restaurants, and hotels of the world. The truth is that it can be just as crucial for a B2B widget manufacturer that no one knows exists.

Hank was one of the first and will forever be among the most unconventional clients I've ever worked with. He was unique because, from the very beginning, he understood the power of exceptional customer service. In fact, he built his business on making every customer interaction sing. He began his career selling extension cords and wire out of his garage. It soon grew into an electronics distribution business and later began manufacturing tiny electronic widgets. Most people don't even know they exist, but these widgets are found in everything electronic. They cost pennies. Hank made millions.

From the beginning, Hank understood the importance of paying attention to details and caring for customers. He approached the manufacture, sales, and support of his little widgets like he was selling a luxury car. The market for his widgets does not have a reputation for stellar customer service. Hank saw this not as an area to contain costs, but as an opportunity to invest in what his competitors never considered. He consistently charged a few pennies more and then made sure that his team took care of their customers better than anyone else in their industry. His company quickly gained a reputation of being the most reliable and trustworthy place to buy these widgets.

For a season, China made a big move into Hank's widget market. The industry panicked as manufacturers chased lower prices and cost savings. I never saw Hank panic. He stayed the course by making a quality product, charging a little more for it, and investing in providing a superior customer experience. For a time, sales dropped as Chinese products made their splash. A year or two later, Hank's company experienced a resurgence in business.

Manufacturers discovered that quality issues with the cheap Chinese widgets caused costly delays. Also, the Chinese companies weren't easy to work with. Orders were commonly late, shipments were missed, and returns were downright impossible. Communication was equally impossible. In the rare instances someone actually picked up a phone, they barely spoke English. Customers suddenly found that the cost savings on the front end often became far more expensive headaches on the back end.

Customers returned to Hank's business in droves. Hank was still there, making sure that his finger was on the pulse of his customers' thoughts and desires. Every representative was trained and accountable for providing an unmatched customer experience.

I assessed and coached Hank's team for almost thirty years. When he finally decided to retire and put his company on the auction block, companies from around the world bid like they were at Christie's bidding on a Van Gogh.

The most inconspicuous businesses can profit from understanding and leveraging the difference between good and great. On the front line of business, it begins with understanding the meaning of quality when it comes to service.

# CHAPTER 3

# Quality

I've watched business fads come and go. While some have had positive effects, I have found others to be regrettable, including one with lingering consequences. For a season, business executives categorized customer support as a "cost center." Customer service was nothing more than a necessary expense, so the key to a successful business was to contain the cost. Do the least that is required. Go through the motions to get the job done. Do it fast and cheap.

It's a short-sighted philosophy. It's the community theater model of business. We don't need to be great, just "good enough."

First, it is a well-established fact that it costs far more to find a new customer than to keep an existing one. Why would you risk losing customers if it's going to cost you more to gain a new one?

Second, every customer interaction is an opportunity to build retention and loyalty. When you create an experience that brings loyal customers back with friends in tow, your support team becomes a source of revenue.

The problem is that getting a hard calculation on that ROI is messy and difficult. It requires a degree of faith to know and experience the return. Bean counters in business don't like messy and difficult calculations. I suspect a bean counter executive created the "customer service is nothing more than a cost center" philosophy in the first place.

Walt Disney wasn't a bean counter. Neither was Steve Jobs at Apple, Tony Hsieh at Zappos, Herb Kelleher at Southwest Airlines, or Howard Schultz at Starbucks. Add my client Hank to that list. These were visionaries who understood that a must-have customer experience was in the details. And by faith they leveraged it into successful businesses that are the stuff of legend.

Instead of counting beans, plant seeds of excellence that will grow your customers' wishes. Have faith and make the investment in your team and your systems. Build your business into one that will have customers buzzing about the difference. Motivate your customers to come back for more.

## Defining Quality: It's More Than Metrics

When number crunching executives get a hold of a business, customers suffer. I saw this happen with an insurance company led by executives bent on starving the customer service cost center. In true bean counter fashion, they reviewed the phone metrics and discovered that the average call was three minutes long. Bean counters love this kind of data to calculate the cost per call and draft a budget forecast.

"The average customer service call is three minutes," they declared to their front-line managers. "Calls shouldn't take longer than three minutes. Make sure your team members keep calls to three minutes or less! All hail average call time and cost containment!"

Armed with their marching orders, the front-line managers applied call metrics to measure the minions. They warned any team members with average call times over three minutes and punished those who didn't obey the executive mandate.

The bean counters didn't see it coming. Agents set their timers. Suddenly, calls lost connection at precisely 2:57. Customer calls were terminated repeatedly. Customers were livid.

That's a true story. The call center that hung up on customers became front-page business news. The bean counters saved pennies on call costs and found themselves spending a lot of dollars learning a very expensive PR lesson. I'd love to know how many customers they had to spend money to replace.

When I explain what I do, many business people proudly inform me they know exactly what I'm talking about.

"Oh yes. Our company does that. We have this software that does that for us."

"It measures service quality?" I ask.

"Sure! It tells us how many calls are answered, the average speed of answer, average call time, and all that data."

At that point, I simply nod and smile. It isn't worthwhile to go any further with the conversation. These people aren't talking about service quality; they're talking about call metrics spit out by their phone system. It's important and useful information, but metrics and call data tell you nothing about the quality of the customer interaction.

Our team regularly produces data around service quality, but it's very different from the output of simple call metrics. It takes work to produce it.

## Measuring Quality Requires Effort

QA was a business fad when it began in the 1990s. For a time, most companies jumped on the bandwagon and started internal QA teams to take advantage of emerging call recording technology. On the surface, it seemed so simple. How hard can it be? You define what you want your people to say and do, then you listen to the call and see if they did it. Companies soon discovered that it's not that easy.

Elizabeth was the senior vice president of a major global financial corporation. She contacted us and asked for a meeting. We joined her in her spacious office in the tower of her company's global headquarters.

"I've got a problem," she announced, "and I hope you can help me."

"We're happy to help. What's the problem?"

Elizabeth proceeded to tell us that all the teams from multiple divisions of the corporation report up to her. All the teams did QA in some form, but they all had the autonomy to do it however they wanted to do it. Each team had internal people tasked with the effort.

I'll never forget Elizabeth chuckling as she shared. She was a very sharp lady.

"Every month I get the QA reports that have been rolled up into a dashboard summary for me. It's always 98 out of 100. Every month it's 98. It never changes. Quite frankly I don't trust it. I don't trust that it's being done consistently. I don't trust that it's being done well. I know human behavior too well. It's not that consistent, and it's not consistently that good!"

Elizabeth asked us to measure all the teams that reported to her using our method. She had reason to be suspicious. Her teams spent a lot of time and energy doing QA, but their methods were rife with problems and inconsistencies. The results were untrustworthy. Our SQA uncovered the issues. For over a decade, we provided Elizabeth with results she could trust to improve customer experience.

Within twenty years of the emerging QA fad, most companies abandoned internal efforts, and QA largely fell out of fashion. Business moved on to new fads. Still, our clients continued paying Intelligentics to be their QA provider. They still do. Our services provide measurable value for them.

So, why did the business world largely abandon the QA effort?

Executives like Elizabeth came to realize that they couldn't trust the results, so they concluded the value didn't justify the investment. For many, it solidified the cost-center mentality, and they regressed to the community theater model of business. They threw warm bodies armed with a few rehearsed lines to perform on the stage of customer interactions, hoping they wouldn't botch things up too badly.

They threw the baby out with the bathwater.

On the surface, QA does appear to be simple. Listen to the call. Was it good or bad? The answer is actually layered in complexity. Doing QA well so that it provides reliable data and actual results requires knowledge, effort, and discipline. In other words, the community theater metaphor is just as applicable to corporate QA as it is to corporate customer service. The difference is in the details.

As Elizabeth experienced with her teams, many internal QA programs that don't work simply need to be nurtured. Call centers can generate revenue when sound methodologies are backed by statistical rigor, unpolluted by internal politics, and implemented with discipline. Discipline must be developed.

# Life Lesson: Knowledge, Effort, and Discipline

Chuck gave me an assignment in our first 6:00 a.m. meeting back in high school. The assignment was to memorize Joshua 1:8 so that I could recite it perfectly the following week.

> *This book of the law shall not depart from your mouth, but you shall meditate on it day and night, so that you may be careful to do according to all that is written in it; for then you will make your way prosperous, and then you will have success.*
> Joshua 1:8 (NASB 1995)

It had been about eighteen months since I had had the vision. I had been traveling with the church choir and preaching for about a year. I was reading my Bible on my own and paying attention at church. I had faith and passion, but I didn't know what I didn't know. And boy, was there a lot I didn't know.

God put Chuck into my life to teach me about knowledge, discipline, and effort. He taught me to meditate on God's word "day and night" and live "according to all that is written in it" every day.

Over two years, Chuck led me through a structured discipleship approach. Others joined us for a time, but it never lasted. They would show up for a week or two and then I wouldn't see them again. After two years, right before I was about to graduate from high school, Chuck took me to one of the best restaurants in the city to celebrate. I had spent two years making the effort to learn what it truly means to be a disciple of Jesus.

The word *disciple* comes from the Latin word *discipulus*, which is translated as *learner, pupil,* or *apprentice.* It comes from the same Latin root word from which we derive the word *discipline.* In Jesus's day, disciples were students who walked in the footsteps of their rabbi's sandals. They followed him. They listened to every word. They wrote those words down (if they could write). They imitated him every day in every way.

In life and ministry, I've observed different types of followers of Jesus. Some show up at church on Sundays the way thousands showed up on the mountainside to hear Jesus teach. Jesus had a large circle of seventy-two people whom He sent out to proclaim His message. Then there were the twelve disciples and four women who were always with Him.

Jesus's closest disciples spent years putting in the effort to develop spiritual discipline and grow in knowledge. What was the difference in outcome? It was a matter of who was left standing when things got most real. Only John and the ladies had the faith and courage to be with Jesus at the cross. The crowd of thousands of followers who showed up to listen and eat the miraculous free filet-o-fish sandwiches was nowhere to be found. As soon as Jesus presented challenging ideas like eating His flesh and drinking His blood, people abandoned Him like a failed business fad (John 6:25–71).

## Quality Is Best Defined by Your Customers

I love working with clients who are new to both customer research and QA. When a business gets inside the heads and hearts of its customers for the first time, the outcomes can be transformational.

One such client was a successful family operation that had been in business for over a century. Multiple generations of the family built and managed a reputable regional brand, but suddenly, they had a problem. Their business had begun to wane. All signs indicated they were not attracting younger generations as customers. We had the honor of doing the first customer research their company had ever done.

The feedback we gathered revealed both hard truths and exciting opportunities. The hard truth was that the customers they knew best and to whom they had successfully marketed for generations were aging. Millennial and Gen Z customers saw our client as a respected brand. They didn't, however, feel like it was "their" type of brand.

The outcome of the study provided our client with a tactical blueprint for marketing to the next generation. They learned what the younger generations thought about the brand, what they didn't like about the company's marketing, and what would speak to them.

Luckily, the younger generation felt a strong positive bond with the brand and its history. Informed by both the strengths and the gaps, our client took advantage of an exciting opportunity to ensure the future of the company. They simply pivoted their marketing to capitalize on their emotional ties with the next generation of customers.

Every business leader defines quality differently. Their definition is revealed by the criteria given to their front-line agents. Bean counters define quality as metrics tied to costs. Visionaries define quality through strong personalities and passionate convictions of what they believe customers should experience. Few companies define quality by learning and delivering on actual customer expectations. That's a mistake.

Both in business and in life, I've learned that the key to success is learning and delivering on others expectations, not my own.

# Life Lesson: Learning and Delivering on My Loved One's Expectations

When I stepped into the bedroom, I felt the chill. It was not the physical chill of winter but a relational chill I had never experienced in our marriage.

My wife Wendy and I have a wonderful marriage. We met in a production at our local community theater. We love the same things in life. We do everything together. We work together in home offices. We serve together in the community. Our recreational activities are done together. We are pretty much with one another 24/7/365. Many people we know confess that they could never do life with their spouse the way we do. It works for us. *C'est la vie.*

But when I walked into the bedroom that night, the chill shook my soul. Something had broken, and I knew that I had to do something about it. I didn't know how, and that terrified me.

Wendy and I were trying to have children. Our daughters from my previous marriage were teenagers when Wendy and I got married. Wendy had never been married before. The desire to have a child together led the two of us on the most difficult journey of my entire life. The road led through medical tests, surgeries, and escalating rounds of fertility treatments.

There is something very real about the path of infertility that cuts into a woman's soul. So much so that the theme resonates repeatedly throughout the Great Story with deep spiritual significance in the stories of Sarah, Hannah, and Elizabeth, to name a few. As a man, I didn't get it, I didn't understand it, and it scared the living daylights out of me.

I eventually learned that Wendy needed me to enter her pain and to grieve with her. She needed me to be present with her in physical, emotional, and spiritual ways I never had before. I had to learn what that meant from Wendy herself. I had to ask God for levels of wisdom and discernment unknown to me. I had to become vulnerable in ways that pushed me way past my established masculine limitations.

We got pregnant once, but the pregnancy ended in miscarriage. Having a baby and raising a child together is not part of our story. Yet our story includes a depth of connection and intimacy far beyond what I knew to be possible.

Paul wrote to Jesus's disciples in Philippi:

> Do nothing out of selfish ambition or vain conceit. Rather, in humility value others above yourselves, not looking to your own interests but each of you to the interests of the others.

In your relationships with one another, have the same mindset as Christ Jesus:

> *Who, being in very nature God,*
> *did not consider equality with God something to*
> *be used to his own advantage;*
> *rather, he made himself nothing*
> *by taking the very nature of a servant,*
> *being made in human likeness.*
> *And being found in appearance as a man,*
> *he humbled himself*
> *by becoming obedient to death—*
> *even death on a cross!*
> Philippians 2:3–8

Successful businesses learn what their customers expect, then they tailor every touchpoint to meet and exceed those expectations.

That's exactly what Jesus did when He left heaven to come to earth and sacrifice Himself for all of humanity, including you and me.

As a disciple of Jesus, walking in the footprints of Jesus's sandals, I should do the same in my relationship with my family, my friends, and my clients. Even when it's hard.

When I do so, the outcomes are out of this world.

## The Holy Trinity of CSAT

The family business from the earlier example will continue to thrive because they tuned into the nuanced expectations of their evolving customer base. The proliferation of communication channels and the drastic generational differences in today's world mean that it is more important than ever for businesses to understand their customers.

However, there are universals to customer satisfaction. I call these foundational drivers of satisfaction the "Holy Trinity of CSAT."

The three elements of the Holy Trinity of CSAT are (in order of importance):

1. Resolution: "Solve my issue or answer my question, preferably in one contact."
2. Courtesy and Friendliness: "Be nice and care about me and my issue/question."
3. Time-Related Dimensions of Service: "Respect my time."

How these three drivers manifest themselves in the particulars of customer expectation can change from client to client. Nevertheless, they are always the foundation on which excellent service is built. It's important to know each one.

## *One-Contact Resolution*

Contact centers have long known that single-contact resolution is goal number one. While management teams in smaller businesses may be unaware, every business should understand the universal rule of one-contact resolution.

Most business leaders fail to consider the negative impact of repeat calls on a customer's overall perception of the business. When we conduct CSAT research for clients, we ask customers how many contacts it took to get their issue resolved. We then compare that to the customer's overall satisfaction rating with the company. While some customers understand and forgive a second call, no one appreciates a company that can't capitalize on second chances. Satisfaction ratings fall significantly if the customer must reach out three or more times. And data suggests that customers are even less tolerant now than they were fifteen years ago. I've seen a growing gap between one-contact and two-contact resolution satisfaction as smartphones reshape culture and customers place more value on speed.

Don't assume that the number of contacts is equal to how many times the customer interacted with a rep. Customers count contacts differently.

Regardless of whether they engage with someone, every time a customer reaches out is a contact. For example, if your Voice Response Unit (VRU) traps customers in a quagmire of loops, then your business has already failed the first contact. Likewise, if an agent promises a call or email back and it never happens, the failed promise is a contact. In the customer's mind, it's a contact that never happened but should have. Therefore, when the customer must initiate another contact, they consider it the third contact. The second contact was the ghost that never materialized. It's the company's fault.

One of the most profitable pieces of data that our SQA surfaces are the repeated situations that drive multiple contacts. If you can reduce those, you not only save the cost of unnecessary contacts but also the customer's diminished satisfaction.

## Courtesy and Friendliness

When approached by a potential client, our team suggests a pilot project to walk through all three touchpoints of our continuous improvement method. First, we run an initial customer satisfaction survey and a one-time Service Quality Assessment (SQA). Comparing the results reveals obvious gaps between customer expectations and customer experience. That data is utilized to present a training event for our client's front-line team. We have the data. We know the gaps. We can provide them with the tactical service skills they need to improve. Sometimes it's as simple as a well-placed courtesy word.

In a pilot SQA, we often listen for the customer to receive a simple *please* or *thank you* from the CSR. In the early years of my career, I found that CSRs used a *please* or *thank you* about half of the time. This was without it even being addressed or discussed. That has changed. One of the lowest demonstrations of this simple courtesy I've witnessed came from a team of twelve CSRs in Iowa. The team was made up of older, small-town, Iowa-nice females. I was shocked when only 8 percent of callers in a pilot assessment heard a *please* or *thank you* from these friendly ladies.

Our culture has become less courteous, and it's only getting worse. This problem is an opportunity for you and your team. Courtesy and friendliness have always been and will always be part of the Holy Trinity of CSAT. The fact that we live in a discourteous culture hasn't changed the human desire for a courteous and personable experience. In fact, our most recent research reveals that call-averse Gen Z actually desires human interaction with businesses in certain situations. The key is to know when and how. If you do, you have an advantage. In today's tech-driven culture, it doesn't take much to differentiate yourself from the inhospitable herd.

## Time-Related Dimensions of Service

For the first fifteen years of my career, the key drivers of the CSAT pie chart only had two pieces. It wasn't yet a CSAT trinity but a CSAT binary. The biggest piece was resolution. The second piece was courtesy and friendliness. The landscape of business changed in 2007 with the introduction of the iPhone. Our lives, including our work and our center of commerce, were suddenly ever-present, right in the palm of our hand. We have instant access to more information than any human beings since the dawn of time. We expect that we can quickly do anything we need to do on our phones. It's changing our expectations of both business and life.

The implications for business are complex. What is universally true is that customers are more cognizant of time. They are less patient than ever. They have demanding expectations for rapid resolution. However, these expectations play out in different dimensions. Specific time-related dimensions of service that matter to customers can differ from client to client. Everything matters, from how easy it is to reach you to how quickly you bring up my account. The impact of every touchpoint can shift dramatically between customer populations.

When it comes to investing in improvement, we all want to know where we are going to get the biggest bang for our buck. Whether you're focused on the general landscape of the Holy Trinity of CSAT or you're digging into the weeds of customer expectations, you want to have maximum impact. To make that determination, it's important to know the difference between reward variables and penalty variables.

## Reward Variables and Penalty Variables

How much will customers reward you for meeting or exceeding their expectations? The elements that drive customer satisfaction are either penalty variables or reward variables.

Penalty variables mean that a customer will penalize you with decreased satisfaction if you fail to meet their expectations. However, they will not reward you with increased levels of satisfaction if you do.

Resolution is a prime example of a penalty variable. The customer is saying, "I expect you to resolve my issue, period. If you don't, I'm not going to be happy. But if you do, I'm not going to suddenly become your raving fan just for doing your job."

Time-related dimensions of service are also penalty variables. Customers expect you to handle issues quickly and efficiently. They expect that from everyone and companies like Amazon have trained them to expect it. There's no reward for doing so. If they feel like you're wasting their time, however, they will not be happy.

Reward variables are the opposite. The more you meet and exceed the customer's expectations on a reward variable, the more the customer rewards you with increasing levels of satisfaction.

Courtesy and friendliness are reward variables. I see this every time I ask a training class to name a company that has great customer service. Chick-fil-A is virtually always Exhibit A. When I ask training participants why Chick-fil-A is known for exceptional customer service, the response is always two words: "My pleasure." When you say "thank you" to any Chick-fil-A team member, the response is always "My pleasure." The company has leveraged an uncommonly courteous two-word response into a national reputation for having great customer service.

Understanding the Holy Trinity of CSAT and both penalty and reward variables is perhaps the most profoundly simple lesson I've learned in my career. It's true in both business and life. There are unlimited rewards awaiting those who consistently demonstrate simple courtesy.

## Life Lesson: The Holy Trinity of CSAT in Everyday Life

Every week, I walk downstairs from my Intelligentics C-suite to find Wendy doing laundry. Wendy designed our house. She created her own "operations suite" on the main floor. Her office, the kitchen, pantry, and laundry room are all within a few feet of one another.

It was well established in the first weeks of marriage that Wendy didn't want me touching the laundry. The org chart of Home Ops at Vander Well Manor clearly has Wendy in control of the laundry silo. I'm listed in a small box at the bottom. I'm allowed limited folding responsibilities and occasional emergency laundry privileges for my own clothing.

The same org chart has my name at the top of anything outside. The lawn, landscaping, and snow removal are my domain here at Vander Well Manor.

Early in our marriage, I began making a point of saying "thank you" to Wendy every time I catch her doing my laundry. Likewise, every time I walk into the house from mowing the lawn, I hear Wendy say "thank you." Why? We realized that the Holy Trinity of CSAT is as applicable in our marriage and our home operations as it is in business.

I've had people tell me, "That's stupid. Why should I thank my spouse for doing the necessary tasks of life?"

We do it because we don't want a neutral marital experience. Even satisfied doesn't cut it with us. I want my wife to be very satisfied with our relationship and our life together. To get to that level of satisfaction, I must go beyond Wendy's marital expectations. She needs to experience the reward variables of marital courtesy and friendliness.

How very simple it is to say "thank you for doing the laundry" every time I catch her doing it. How subtly satisfying it is to hear Wendy say "thank you" when I'm sweaty and gross from doing mundane lawn care. Those seeds of gratitude germinate over time. They plant relational roots. They produce the fruit of mutual appreciation. That fruit is essential to the great relationship Wendy and I enjoy.

*Little children, let us stop just saying we love
people; let us really love them, and show it by
our actions.* 1 John 3:18 (TLB)

When I was a teenager, I chose 1 John 3:18, Philippians 4:6–7, and Proverbs 3:5–6 to guide my life. As a college graduation gift, my brother wrote all three of my life verses in different styles of beautiful calligraphy. He had it framed for me. Today, if you step into my office, it's the first thing you see staring right at you.

Even as a young man, I wanted my faith to be more than just a membership certificate from my local church. Being a disciple of Jesus informs everything I do and how I treat others.

As I presented research to clients repeatedly, it became clear to me that the Holy Trinity of CSAT is a human universal. Every human being wants these things. As I meditated, I realized that if it's true in business, then it's true in other human interactions. It's why Wendy and I express courtesy to one another, even for the mundane tasks of everyday life.

I say "I love you" to Wendy every day, multiple times a day. But how do I apply my life verse and show her through my actions? Why shouldn't the Holy Trinity of CSAT be just as effective as the "Holy Trinity of WSAT" (wife's satisfaction) or "KSAT" (kid satisfaction) or "FSAT" (friend satisfaction)?

I confess that my ability to apply this remains a work in progress. Wendy will be happy to give you examples. Like business, sometimes change takes time and consistent effort. It helps to start small with a pilot project, make a few prioritized changes, then start building on those positive changes.

## It's Complicated

The Holy Trinity of CSAT provides a universal foundation upon which to build a strong customer experience. Remember, however, that the difference between good and great is in the details. What you build on top of that foundation gets more complicated based on the unique customer base your business serves.

A private equity firm bought two companies that manufactured and sold the same electronic component. The CMO was tasked with building a unified website to improve the digital experience for the customers of both companies. That was going to be a challenge.

The customer bases of the companies' products were vastly different. One company designed, manufactured, and sold a basic standard version. Their customers were low-end manufacturers and hobbyists working out of their homes. The other company dealt with the most complex and high-end components ever made. Their customer base included NASA, defense contractors, and the military.

Suddenly, the idea of merging two companies making the same type of component became very complex. Our team designed a VOC project for each customer base to understand its expectations. Our client then used the data to design a website and online customer portal that would work successfully for both.

Business happens in all shapes and sizes. Customer and client bases are equally diverse. This is one of the things I've loved experiencing in my career. There are nuances specific to different business and customer markets of all sizes. For example, one client is a marketing agency with fewer than fifty active clients. With such a focused client list, the client relationships are intimate. Because of this, clients are sometimes afraid to provide feedback. They want to be brutally honest, but they don't want to jeopardize the relationship. In these cases, we get honest feedback through confidential qualitative interviews. Clients even admit they would never have shared the feedback with the agency directly for fear of hurting the relationship. Two years later, the agency owner shared with me that his team still relies on all they learned about their clients' expectations from that study.

As I touched on earlier, generational differences present another challenge. Generational differences have always existed. However, they've never been as pronounced as they are in our current marketplace. Millennials and Gen Z think and behave in ways that their elders struggle to understand. The two generations are also extremely different. These differences influence marketing, communication, and expectations throughout the customer journey.

Your customer profile, your industry, and the market in which you operate all influence the expectations of your customer base. The better you know those differences, the more effective your operational decisions will be in improving satisfaction, loyalty, and retention.

## Life Lesson: Understanding the Unique Needs of Loved Ones

*"My son," the father said, "you are always with me, and everything I have is yours. But we had to celebrate and be glad, because this brother of yours was dead and is alive again; he was lost and is found." Luke 15:31–32*

*Take your pay and go. I want to give the one who was hired last the same as I gave you. Don't I have the right to do what I want with my own money? Or are you envious because I am generous? Matthew 20:14–15*

*Jesus answered (Peter), "If I want him to remain alive until I return, what is that to you? You must follow me." John 21:22*

"Dad, I have a question for you," my older daughter said.

I've enjoyed daddy-daughter dates with my girls since they were little. This was one I'll never ever forget. We were in a coffee shop here in our little town of Pella, Iowa. Taylor was about sixteen. Her question rocked me to my soul.

"If God hates divorce, then why are you and Mom both so much happier since you split?"

Oh my. I wasn't expecting that. Taylor is my eldest. Even then, she was an old soul. Her thoughts and emotions have always been still waters that run deep.

The question unlocked an intimate and important conversation about life and relationships. On one level, it was about a young woman seeing her parents as individuals. On a deeper level, it was about her starting to consider the complex mix of experiences, traits, and needs that people bring to relationships.

As a certified Enneagram coach, I help leaders see each team member's Enneagram type and how it shapes communication, coping, and conflict. It has transformed teams by turning frustration into understanding and conflict into dialogue.

I have found the Enneagram to be even more important in the context of family and friends. Ironically, it was our old soul daughter Taylor who introduced Wendy and me to the Enneagram many years ago. Understanding each other's Enneagram types allows us to appreciate one another's differences in the ways we think and behave. It's improved our marriage and our family relationships.

As my spiritual journey deepened, I grew to appreciate that God gave every person unique fingerprints. Human beings love to paint humanity with broad brushes as if we're all the same. We then reason that we should think and behave the same and have the same outcomes.

Jesus continuously revealed that the economy of God's kingdom doesn't work that way. Let me give you three examples.

In the parable of the prodigal son, Jesus reveals a father with two boys who couldn't have been more different from one another. The father not only sees this, but it changes the way he parents and communicates with each son.

In the parable of the workers in the vineyard, a vineyard owner hires successive groups of workers throughout the course of a day. With each group, he negotiates the same total wage for what amounts to shorter work hours. The last shift made a lot more per hour than those who were hired early in the morning. The early morning shift cries foul, but the vineyard owner points out that they agreed to the wage, and it's his money to spend as he chooses.

After Jesus's resurrection, He meets the disciples on the shore of the Sea of Galilee. He restores Peter's position of leadership in the organization after Peter's tragic denials on the night of Jesus's arrest. Jesus then informs Peter that his position of leadership and his accepting of the job are going to ultimately cost him his earthly life. Peter's earthly journey will end the same way Jesus's earthly life ended. Peter's reaction to this news is so very human. He glances at John and asks Jesus, "What about him?"

"What's it to you?" Jesus replies. John and Peter had different temperaments, gifts, and strengths, so Jesus had different missions for each of them.

It's a very human trait to want everything to be the same for everyone. We desire equity in all things. We want this earthly life to be fair.

It's not. Father God sees each of us as His unique child. Our relationship with Him is likewise personal and different. His purpose and plan for each of us on this earthly journey is distinct.

The more I seek to understand people, then the better equipped I am to love them well.

## Internal Customers Are Customers Too

I recently received one of the most welcome calls of my career. It was from a client the Intelligentics team has worked with for over ten years. Our continuous improvement model of research, SQA, and training helped our client reach consistently high levels of service performance and customer satisfaction across three customer-facing teams. The call was from the manager of a small team of five back-room team members. The team was not customer-facing, but front-line CSRs called upon the team to assist with accounting or technical problems.

"Our CSRs and techs are our customers," she told me. "If we don't care for them as well as they care for our customers, then the customer experience suffers."

She asked me for a proposal to add her team to the company's SQA program. She wanted her team to be trained and held accountable to the same service standards as everyone else.

That's the sign of a company that is doing more than paying lip service to the customer experience. When multiple teams must fix a customer's issue, it becomes harder to deliver an exceptional experience. Team members must follow certain steps in communication, and each one is a threat of breakdown.

When more than one operational team is required to resolve the customer's issue, the odds of maintaining an exceptional customer experience get longer. Certain steps of communication must happen between team members. Each of those communication touchpoints is an opportunity for things to go wrong. It also requires that team members with no customer connection must care about the customer and their colleagues. Far too often, this is where destructive attitudes take root.

"Why should I care about customer service? I never talk to the customer!"

"QA doesn't apply to me, and neither do all those phone skills."

I run into these attitudes when our team provides QA for internal teams such as tech support and operations support. It makes me sad, but I've seen individuals on these teams quit or transfer rather than be held accountable for providing good service to their colleagues.

Intelligentics was the QA provider for an entire financial services company for almost twenty-five years. A handful of associates so embodied the "This doesn't apply to me" attitude that they switched positions to avoid accountability and coaching. Since it was a company with a long reputation for brand excellence, it became increasingly difficult for them to avoid it. Eventually, all the individuals with this attitude ended up on a small team together.

If your business has teams on which its front-line associates depend, I guarantee that some of the back-end team members have an ambivalent attitude toward customer service. I also guarantee they are short-circuiting your front-line associates' efforts and making their jobs more difficult.

Companies with consistently great customer service understand that the customer experience is a company-wide mission that requires all team members to care about both their internal and external customers.

Once again, this is not just a lesson about business, but an important lesson about life.

## Life Lesson: My Personal Internal Customers

*Children, obey your parents in the Lord, for this is right.* Ephesians 6:1

*Fathers, do not embitter your children, or they will become discouraged.* Colossians 3:21

I joined my mother in the kitchen to ask for permission to attend a weekend trip with some friends. It was my freshman year of high school, just a few months after I asked Jesus to be the Lord of my life. I don't recall the reason, but I remember my mother immediately telling me that I couldn't go on the trip. Her look, her tone, and her posture were all defensive. Every part of her being was prepped for the battle in anticipation of a full teen tirade and accusations of parental abuse.

I shrugged at her and nodded.

"Okay," I simply said before calmly turning and walking back to my room.

I can still see and feel how stunned she was in that moment.

When my sister and I became disciples of Jesus back in our teen years, it transformed our lives. We began to think and behave differently than we had before. God showed me that my attitude, words, and behavior toward my loved ones had to change. I made every effort to put the direct instruction, "Children, obey your parents," into practice. My sister did the same.

Within months, my parents wondered what had happened to their children. They both made personal commitments to Jesus. Our lives were changing, not just in public, but in the privacy of our own homes and family systems.

In his prison letters to the believers in Ephesus and Colossae, Paul was careful to give direct instructions to all family members. The implication is so simple and clear, but I find it is often overlooked. Faith, love, and obedience to Jesus begin at home. Our lives are concentric circles of relationships, and the inner circle is made up of our family.

I've seen many walk away from faith because their parents posed as righteous in church but ruled the home with anger and control. After an entire childhood of experiencing the hypocritical contrast, I understand why they would walk away.

Throughout God's Great Story, I find that transformation always begins with a makeover of attitudes and actions from the inside out. It was that way with Paul. It was that way with me and my family. It's that way with marriage. It's that way with business. Whether in business or family, familiarity should never be an excuse to treat one another poorly. It should be motivation to treat one another with more honor and respect than those in the larger concentric circles of our influence.

# CHAPTER 4

# How Call Monitoring and QA Work

It was 1994. I visited a client's contact center on my first day as Chuck's employee. Hundreds of agents were taking orders and resolving issues for a national catalog retailer. I was escorted into one of those mechanical closets that every office building has, but no one enters. No one knows what's in there.

This closet contained a wall panel with hundreds of analog phone jacks. Each jack corresponded to a different agent's desk. We stuck one end of a cord into a phone jack and the other end into a cassette tape recorder. Then we waited for the associate to take a call. When the phone was answered we pressed the *Record* button.

This is where QA began. Intelligentics had a team of associates who spent hours inside closets at tiny, makeshift desks with clipboards, phone cords, and cassette recorders. It was a manual, time-consuming process. For years, my desk was littered with stacks of cassette tapes. A Sony Walkman was my friend.

Voice-activated cassette recorders transformed the process. Then digital recorders came along. Eventually, Voice Over IP (VoIP) technology made digital recording, storage, and access to calls easy for virtually any business. There have been so many changes as the QA fad waxed and waned. I learned many lessons along the journey. While the tools have changed dramatically, the core purpose of QA has not: to tell the truth about the customer experience and help people grow.

## Let's Go to the Tape—Recordings Don't Lie

She sat across from me in a small corporate conference room. Everything about her was a silent scream that she didn't want to be there. Her stiff posture, crossed arms, refusal to make eye contact, and curt responses told me I had my work cut out for me.

The data from our assessments revealed that the woman never used the customer's name during her calls. It was one of the QA criteria we measured. It's a simple way to introduce a little friendliness into a customer interaction. Just use the caller's name once in a conversational way. She stared at the floor while we listened to a call. When the recording ended, I asked what she thought she did well, and what she might have improved.

"It was perfect," she blurted.

This was going to be even harder than I expected.

"Well, I noticed that you didn't use the customer's name in the call."

"I did," she shot back at me.

"You did?"

"I did," she demanded.

I smiled and nodded. "Okay. I'm going to play the call again. Please point out to me the point at which you use the customer's name."

I played the call again. She remained silent in oppositional defiance.

I'm happy to say coaching sessions like that are rare, but it reminds me of the power of call monitoring. The recording doesn't lie. It's a friend to those who wish to improve. It's a mirror for those who don't.

The difference between good and great is in the details. Consider professional athletes. Pay attention the next time you watch a professional baseball or football game. The first thing players do after a play is watch the recording. Football teams pour over the recording of their previous game in the days after a game. They break down every play, every tackle, every moment. Baseball players look at every pitch and every swing. Then they do the same with recordings of their next opponent.

The recording reveals a path to better outcomes. Sales associates discover missed opportunities to ask about the customer's pain points. CSRs learn the most effective ways to express empathy and drive the call toward resolution. Every escalated customer issue is rooted in a communication problem. The best way to address the problem is by going to the tape, the email thread, or the chat transcription.

The most common complaint I hear from associates is, "I hate listening to myself." The second most common complaint is, "I can't believe I missed that. I feel like I say that on every call!"

I know they strive for consistency. QA data reveals they are successful most of the time. But not all the time. The key to great customer service is to approach the job like a professional baseball player trying to improve his batting average.

Go to the tape, identify opportunities, and keep swinging.

The first thing every quarterback does after an interception is watch the video to see what defensive coverage he missed. But the line coach reviews the video to determine why the quarterback was under such pressure in the first place. And the offensive coordinator looks at the same video to determine whether he should have called a different play.

In the same way, the rewards and consequences for QA go beyond the performance of individual team members. A strong QA process examines more than what a CSR said and how they said it. It analyzes calls from the customer's perspective. It considers the situation and the circumstances that drove the call in the first place. It spots improvement opportunities across the business.

One of our company's legendary stories is that of a major satellite broadcasting company we served. One month, our QA team identified an unusual spike in calls from customers whose service had been turned off for non-payment. Angry customers claimed they had paid on time. CSRs confirmed their spotless payment records. So why were we hearing so many of these calls in a single month?

The vice president of operations confirmed our findings and initiated an investigation. The inquiry showed their lockbox provider was holding customers' checks instead of processing them. The client calculated that our prompt reporting saved him at least $100,000 in unnecessary calls, not to mention the incalculable damage to customer satisfaction and customer loss.

Issues involving systems, security, shipping, scheduling, internal communication, and products all fester, waiting to be identified. Once fixed, the customers and the company benefit from a productive system that delivers a smooth experience. It's all on the tape, if you know how to break it down, listen to it, and learn from the data.

The same data will eventually reveal the improvement. I love to watch clients as they see their service quality performance improve. For the very first time, they can quantify that their team is delivering on the mission and brand promise. Their confidence grows.

They also have actual data on which to reward individuals and teams for their good performance and to identify areas of opportunity. Great performers are finally recognized and rewarded for the good job they do every day. Poor performers are finally held accountable, and they are equipped and trained to step up. The process identifies exactly what they need to do.

Customers notice a consistently better experience every time they call. Data from our annual CSAT survey reveals increasing levels of satisfaction. Costs diminish from gains in efficiency and resolution. Sales increase from greater levels of loyalty and retention.

Go to the tape. It doesn't lie. It contains information that can transform your business. It can help take you to a whole new level of success. Of course, this requires that the tape is analyzed in a productive and profitable way. That's not always a given. Sometimes the same content can be analyzed in very different ways. Some methods aren't as effective.

## Objective and Subjective QA

As QA grew as a business fad back in the 1990s, many companies applied a frugal DIY mentality. The C-suites assumed it can't be hard to grade call quality, and appointed team leaders to figure it out. Across business, methods emerged that ranged from subjective to rigid legalism.

Those who adopted subjective methods allowed managers to make their own personal value judgments. The result was internal chaos. Every supervisor had their own criteria and biases. Analysis was haphazard, inconsistent, and had little measurable value.

I observed some companies attempting to bring a little structure to the subjective free-for-all. One company I audited had three questions that every manager answered in evaluating a call's quality:

1. Was the issue resolved?
2. Did the team member reflect our brand promise?
3. Did we delight the customer?

This approach wasn't much better than letting the supervisors go it alone because there were no definitions or criteria to guide them. Supervisors listened to the same call and gave completely different answers:

*Was the issue resolved?*

Supervisor Bob says, "Yes. The customer asked a question. The CSR agreed to find out and call him back. Resolved."

Supervisor Megan says, "No! It's not resolved until the customer gets the return call."

*Did the team member reflect our brand promise?*

Manager Shawntae says, "Yes. Our brand promise is to deliver, and we're going to do that when we call the customer back."

Manager Eric says, "No. We didn't deliver. The team member could have placed the caller on hold, found the answer, and resolved it in one call."

*Did we delight the customer?*

Supervisor Chris says, "Yes. The customer seemed delighted to me."

Manager Michael says, "No. We used the customer's name only once. The team member could have delighted the customer more by using it another time."

You can see the differences and discrepancies that lead to inconsistent outcomes. On the surface, the subjective approach appears easy but it fails to measure and drive consistent, measurable outcomes.

It didn't take long for front-line associates to realize their QA results were subjective and based on supervisor bias. The results were as different as the supervisor who scored the calls.

Managers soon realized that the process wasn't creating any kind of positive change. Supervisors always have more pressing priorities than analyzing calls. Analyzing calls can be tedious. So it just didn't get done. Management eventually concluded that QA doesn't work and abandoned the effort. The baby got thrown out with the bathwater.

On the other end of the spectrum were companies that built obsessive, legalistic methods to define expectations. They measured every word and analyzed boatloads of phone calls. One client I audited created a "definition document" as a guide for internal analysts and CSRs. The document was more than 300 pages long. Calibration sessions became heated debates about the interpretation of the criteria on page 173, paragraph 3, section B, subsection 5c. The number of calls assessed per associate was equally extreme.

Though far from the subjective approach, the rigid legalistic one proved just as disastrous. CSRs were burdened by over 300 pages of detailed expectations. Coaching sessions became trials. Calibration sessions descended into heated debates. A multi-layer court of appeals developed for arguing QA scores. You might also notice that the customer has been lost in the quagmire of corporate QA bureaucracy.

Being the man in the middle, I discovered that truth is found at the point of tension between the two extremes. An effective QA method balances sound judgment and meaningful criteria. Let me share with you the most effective ways to do that. It begins with ensuring that those analyzing customer interactions can and will do so objectively.

## Objective Analysts

A corporate senior vice president called and asked me if I would perform an audit of his company's internal QA process. He loved his team, but suspected the quality reports weren't accurate. We agreed to compare the graded results of the same calls using their internal process alongside Intelligentics' standard method. I took a good look at their internal processes and recent reports.

There were three teams in the internal QA program. A supervisor from each team analyzed calls using criteria the management team had established. As I reviewed the most recent data, I discovered the tech support team appeared to be service quality rock stars. Immediately my internal alarms went off because, as a general rule, our SQA reveals that tech support teams often struggle with customer care. Tech Support Representatives (TSRs) have knowledge about technology but may lack nuanced communication skills. The more skilled a TSR is, the easier it is to forget that customers' basic tech knowledge falls far below theirs. I wanted to reserve judgment, however. Maybe the client's team was the exception, not the rule. It was time to go to the tape and review the calls. The recording doesn't lie.

The data from our audit and assesment revealed two things. First, the client's scoring method was so flawed that every team's results were falsely inflated. (I'll explain how a bit later.) Even more concerning was the tech support supervisor giving reps credit for criteria they didn't meet. This prompted a conversation between me and the department manager. I asked if the teams' QA results were tied to any kind of financial incentive. They were. The company let supervisors score their own team's calls and then paid them a bonus for good results.

This episode is a microcosm of why many internal QA efforts failed. When internal team members evaluate their colleagues, two personas of bias emerge. These personas reflect the extremes of the subjective and objective.

Let's call the first persona the "Cheerleader." The Cheerleader is a well-intentioned QA analyst who is the ever-cheerful optimist. They want everyone to get along and be happy. They want to avoid conflict at all costs. They see good in people. So much so, in fact, that they often choose not to score team members objectively. The

Cheerleader feels guilty withholding any points. Instead, they think, "I'm sure they meant to do it. They usually don't miss that. I'll just give them credit and coach them on it." As soon as this happens, however, the Cheerleader has introduced noise into the QA data. The resulting data is not an accurate reflection of reality. It's an accurate reflection of the Cheerleader's optimistic view of what should have been.

Opposite of the Cheerleader is what I call the Heated Blacksmith. A Blacksmith believes that iron sharpens iron. Their tools are heat and a hammer. In their minds, every evaluation is a forge, and every team member is raw steel.

Blacksmiths may see themselves as craftsmen, convinced that quality is achieved through pressure, fire, and repeated strikes. Their tough-love approach comes from a belief that a blade tested in the forge will endure.

But equal danger accompanies the Heated Blacksmith. Instead of carefully tempering the blade, the Heated Blacksmith can pound away until they see flaws where none exist. They treat the QA process less like refinement and more like punishment. They swing the hammer not to strengthen but to break. If they dislike a colleague or want to settle a score, the forge becomes a place of vengeance. Zero tolerance, maximum sting.

I remember my first day working with a client's new QA manager. I had noticed that one of the calls she scored was 0 out of a possible 100 points. Based on our methodology, the only way this was even possible would be if the CSR picked up the phone and immediately hung up without saying a word. When I asked the new QA manager about her score of the call, I immediately recognized I was dealing with a Heated Blacksmith.

"Oh!" she exclaimed. "The call was terrible. I couldn't stand it. About halfway through, I just marked the whole thing ZERO!"

The Cheerleader waves her pompons and gives the CSR credit for something they didn't do. This was the opposite. This Heated Blacksmith swung her hammer and eliminated any credit for anything the CSR did in the call. The result is the same. Data that doesn't reflect reality.

Just as a blade can be ruined by over-hammering, a team's QA data becomes warped when a Heated Blacksmith takes control. Their evaluations stop being about accuracy and start being about domination.

Let's be honest. We all need Cheerleaders in our lives. We all need encouragement. We need people who believe in us. We also need Blacksmiths. We have sharp edges and flaws that need a little heat, a little pressure, and we need a craftsman to help fix what's broken. We need Cheerleaders and Blacksmiths in the right proportions at the right times. In other words, you need a man in the middle objectively holiding the tension between the two extremes.

At Intelligentics, we focus on customer-centered systems. Our bias is toward the customer. When we evaluate our clients' calls, we embrace one persona and we are laser-focused. We do the research so we know who our client's customers are and what drives their satisfaction. Then, we apply that knowledge in our analysis of the client's customer interactions.

Our analysts don't know the client's front-line agents. We don't work with them every day. We have no conflicts to avoid or motivations to make them like us. We slip our feet into the customer's shoes and approach our job accordingly.

It should also be noted that internal versus external QA is not an "either-or" proposition. There are "both-and" solutions. My experience is that they can be very effective. Intelligentics has designed, implemented, and administered our clients' QA programs. We train and use the clients' internal analysts. They provide us with enhanced knowledge of the policies, procedures, and systems needed to serve them well. In turn, we bring expertise, objectivity, and analytical discipline. We recognize and help the internal Cheerleaders and Heated Blacksmiths find the tension between the extremes.

## Life Lesson: Everyday Cheerleaders and Heated Blacksmiths

*Fathers, do not exasperate your children; instead, bring them up in the training and instruction of the Lord. Ephesians 6:4*

*Husbands, love your wives, just as Christ loved the
church and gave himself up for her.*
Ephesians 5:25

Family dinners are tough when teens and parents have busy lives and too many activities on the calendar. When my girls were teens, Wendy and I mandated one weekly evening family meal together. Looking back, it was one of the best disciplines we maintained for our family. I was always surprised by the conversations that surfaced when we turned the technology off and shared a meal together.

"Dad? I wanted to thank you for something," my daughter said one evening.

"Yeah? What's that?"

"I want to thank you for trusting us," she answered.

If I recall correctly, Wendy served the assist in picking my jaw up off the dining table. Our daughter continued.

"Our friends' parents just assume their kids are awful, and that they're secretly running around doing terrible things. They treat them like prisoners who can't be trusted and never let them do anything. Their parents always tell them, "No." They won't let them do anything. You've never been like that. So, thank you."

In their tween years, I told our daughters that I wanted to give them the gift of my trust. I promised that when they asked to do things, my default answer would be *yes*. I answered no only if there was a genuine, compelling reason. I trusted them to do the right thing, to be wise, and to make good choices the way we raised them. I then explained how things would change the moment trust was betrayed. I assured them they would not enjoy life if that happened.

I have observed that the spectrum between the lenient Cheerleader and punitive Blacksmith is equally present in other areas of life. In churches, it presents itself in ranges from rose-colored, watered-down religion to harsh, fundamentalist legalism. The spectrum also exists in parenting, marriages, coaching, and in workplace management.

Truth is found at the point of tension between the two extremes. At work, I use objective data to set performance levels and coaching strategies, not unbridled freedom or harsh rule-keeping. I let the same principle guide my parenting.

It wasn't a free-for-all. Wendy and I were engaged with our daughters. I had regular daddy-daughter dates with both of them, and there was a constant flow of bonding and communication. I kept my default to *yes* when the girls asked to do something.

It wasn't always easy. When our youngest daughter was thirteen and she asked to go on a mission trip to Bangkok, the sex-traffic capital of the world, I seriously bit my tongue. After learning the cost of the trip, I concocted a lock-tight strategy to both keep my promise and my little girl safely at home. I told her she could go if she raised the money herself by the tight deadline. She raised all she needed in 72 hours. She went to Thailand, came home in one piece, and God authored a life-altering chapter in her emerging life story.

There were only a handful of moments with each daughter in which my trust was ever tested. None of them were tremendously serious. In the end, I believe that holding the balance of trust required something from both sides of the relationship. When tested, it helped facilitate good communication to maintain a healthy balance.

Time and again, I've observed people pulling toward either extreme of the Cheerleader or the Heated Blacksmith sides of the spectrum. I thank God for the wisdom and peace to be the man in the middle, balancing tension between the two extremes.

## Framework Criteria

In its simplest form, QA is an established set of behavioral criteria. Customer interactions are reviewed to determine whether the criteria were present in the interaction. Of course, that criterion must be established.

The Cheerleader–Heated Blacksmith spectrum can also shape the criteria QA teams use in customer interactions. In companies with Cheerleaders in charge, the criteria might consist of a small handful of subjective questions. However, where Heated Blacksmiths dominate, I might find an exhaustive QA manual of behavioral rules and accompanying mandatory expectations. In either extreme, the customer tends to be a secondary consideration.

A key reason our continuous improvement cycle works so well is that each step of the process feeds and informs the others. We create a custom QA scorecard for every client. We start with what the research says about their customers' expectations. We listen to phone calls to get an understanding of the basic flow of most interactions. Then we start with the foundation of the Holy Trinity of CSAT and construct the QA framework. Data from the customer survey becomes the framing on top of the foundation. The results of both the survey and the QA then feed the writing, production, and content of our client's training.

When consulting clients on effective QA, I bring with me an empty 8x10 picture frame. I hold the empty frame to my face and explain that it is what good QA criteria looks like. It provides a solid framework for the customer experience. But the CSR should be able to be themselves within that frame. They should be able to put their own personality and individual spin on how to present the framework elements.

Good QA criteria is not a word-for-word script. It's a conversational outline. It provides CSRs with established expectations. It should afford them the ability to make it conversational in their own style. The framework must be present, but the CSRs choose whether their frame will be metal, oak, walnut, plastic, or gilded gold.

Take the customer greeting, for example. Many years ago, RadioShack mandated that every employee in America answer the phone with the same greeting. They were to say the exact scripted words:

"Thanks for calling RadioShack. You've got questions. We've got answers. My name is Gregory. How may I help you today?"

I understand the motivation of the marketing and branding Blacksmith who drove that decision. They were eager to use every opportunity to push the corporate brand message to customers. The decision was, however, company-centered. The greeting was long and wordy. It placed a burden on customers to have to sit and listen to the whole thing. Customers got impatient. RadioShack associates began spewing it out as quickly as possible. The whole thing became unintelligible. Customers penalized RadioShack for wasting their time and delaying the resolution they called for. The greeting never received the reward in customer satisfaction RadioShack wanted. A regurgitated, robotic script isn't courteous or friendly. By the way, RadioShack disappeared from the forefront of American business.

In comparison, the criteria for a greeting on an Intelligentics-created scorecard might look something like this:

- Identify the company.
- Identify yourself.
- Ask an inviting question.

There are many ways to personalize this behavioral framework.

"Good morning. Acme Anvils. This is Wylie. How may I help you?"

"Acme Anvils. Wylie speaking. What can I do for you?"

"Acme Anvils, this is Wylie. Who do I have the pleasure of speaking with?"

"This is Wylie with Acme Anvils. May I have your name, please?"

"It's a great day at Acme Anvils. My name is Wylie. How may I assist you?"

When we understand what drives satisfaction, we can build a behavioral framework for every phase of the customer interaction. With the framework in place, we layer soft skills like courtesy, empathy, professionalism, and communication on top. Whatever criteria we come up with, there is one that's non-negotiable. It must be behavioral.

### Behavioral Criteria

Effective QA does not try to discern the motivation, perception, intention, or thought of either the associate or the customer. We're measuring what the agent said and how they said it. We're measuring what they wrote and how they wrote it. The person evaluating the interaction must be able to say either, "Yes, they did it" or "They should have done it but failed to do so."

When I see a QA scorecard with anything beyond a binary *yes* or *no* rating system, the alarms sound. I have seen clients using scoring systems used in surveys.

"On a scale of 1–5 (where 5 is excellent and 1 is unacceptable), rate the CSR on providing a courteous experience for the customer."

This method of QA isn't measuring a CSR's performance. It's measuring the evaluator's opinion of the CSR's performance. If the Cheerleader is on the case, the results will be high, as the Cheerleader muses, "Five! Five! Five! I just love her. She does such a good job and is such an excellent person. Besides, anything less than a four might hurt her self-esteem. That would have a negative ripple effect on the rest of her work."

Any CSR unfortunate enough to have the Heated Blacksmith score their calls will be lucky to crack a 3 on anything. The Heated Blacksmith will explain their rating this way:

"Look, it says 3 is *average*. Most everything I hear in a call is *average*. It's what I hear on every call. It's what every customer hears on every call. *Average* should be the default on everything. If I identify something that could be better, I'm going to give it a *below average*. If I hear something I don't normally hear, I'll give it a 4. It takes something extraordinary to give it a 5."

QA should give associates a clear view of how well they deliver a quality customer experience. Measuring what a person thought about the CSR's performance is not QA, it's a survey of internal opinions.

At this point, you might be asking "Yeah, but Tom? How do you measure courtesy? Isn't it always subjective?"

Not necessarily. Our team has learned what factors into the customer's perception of service elements like courtesy. Customers like it when they have a personal service experience. *Personal* is defined by an agent conversationally using their name during the call. An agent who says "please" and "thank you" will stand out as being courteous in an increasingly discourteous world. An inviting question like, "How may I assist you?" opens a metaphorical door and welcomes the customer into the call. Likewise, an ending salutation like "I hope you have a great day today!" provides a friendly bookend to the call. Each of these is a behavioral element that contributes to a customer's perception of a courteous service experience.

So, now we have four behavioral criteria that push the customer's satisfaction buttons. Let's list them in the order of when they usually happen within the customer conversation.

- Did the CSR provide an inviting question in the greeting? Yes or No?
- Did the CSR say "please" or "thank you" when requesting information? Yes or No?
- Did the CSR conversationally use the caller's name? Yes or No?
- Did the CSR provide a friendly closing salutation? Yes or No?

Now we have four behavioral elements that form a framework for a consistent, courteous customer experience. It also allows CSRs the freedom to express each piece of the framework in their own style.

## Life Lesson: Behavioral Criteria and Me

The acts of the flesh are obvious: sexual immorality, impurity and debauchery; idolatry and witchcraft; hatred, discord, jealousy, fits of rage, selfish ambition, dissensions, factions and envy; drunkenness, orgies, and the like. I warn you, as I did before, that those who live like this will not inherit the kingdom of God.

*But the fruit of the Spirit is love, joy,
peace, forbearance, kindness, goodness,
faithfulness, gentleness and self-control. Against
such things there is no law.*
Galatians 5:19–22

I have a loved one who is a Christian. They are also a perfectionist. They see the world in stark black-and-white terms. They are one of life's Heated Blacksmiths. There is not a CSR on earth who meets their level of expectation. Every time I see them, I hear about the "idiot" they had to deal with on the phone. This inevitably leads to a proud retelling of how they wielded their hammer. The poor agent was subjected to a self-justified, rude, sarcastic, or demeaning remark.

Listening to this repeated pattern of conversation, I wonder which "fruit of the Spirit" my loved one presented to the poor CSR.

I have spent my career on the business side of customer interactions. Front-line associates are required to put up with customers like the loved one I just described. It's the job.

The world of QA has made me see life and relationships outside of business differently. As a follower of Jesus, I am required to put up with people like my loved one. I'm also required to respond to them differently than I observe them reacting. I've come to realize that Paul's list of the acts of the flesh and fruits of the Spirit are God's QA criteria for life. I took a good look at the criteria in the context of my professional experience.

I observe that the institutional church tends to pay attention to certain behavioral criteria more than others. It's the Heated Blacksmith choosing what flaws they choose to hammer while ignoring others. As a kid, I heard many messages at church about the evils of sex, drugs, rock music, and Dungeons & Dragons. I don't recall many lessons about selfish ambition, jealousy, envy, hatred, and discord. I wish I had. It took me most of my life to realize one of the roughest edges of my life.

One day at the store, I felt sudden, intense anger when I saw a certain celebrity on a magazine cover. I was sick of seeing this person's face everywhere I went. I was sick of everyone saying how great this person was. Every time I heard this person's name, I felt a secret inner rage. It's not like me.

As I meditated on this negative reaction, I realized that it wasn't just this one person. This was a recurring emotion toward certain individuals in popular culture that I don't even know. Why was I feeling this intense negative emotion? Anger isn't constructive. So, I dug into it, analyzed it, and broke it down. I'm ashamed to tell you what I discovered about myself.

I have a problem with envy.

I was angry that this person was wildly successful as the world defines it, and I'm not. This person is admired by millions of people in ways I secretly wish I was admired. They have the influence I wish I had. I was envious of this person's fame. I was so angry that I seethed with an inner hatred toward them.

I tweeted my frustration in the moment. The person actually read my tweet and replied. They acknowledged that their success and fame was, indeed, ridiculous. "Even I'm sick of me," they replied. They were humble and had a humor about their success. I was the one with the problem.

So, which fruit of the Spirit was I demonstrating in the Walmart checkout line, feeling all this anger and hatred?

I was about fifty years old when I discovered my blind spot with envy. I'm ashamed to admit my silly struggle. I'm also glad it came to light. Now that I recognize it, I can consciously address it the moment I feel it. I can choose to let it go and ask God to help me with my fame-trap selfish desires. I can choose to be patient and content with the story God is authoring in and through me.

The basic framework of QA is not just about business. In fact, it's God's design. It works in everyday life and relationships. At the end of every day, I can evaluate my behavior toward Wendy, a colleague, or the disembodied voice of a CSR. Which of God's behavioral QA criteria best describes my words and behaviors toward any one of them?

| | |
|---|---|
| Love | Hatred |
| Joy | Discord |
| Peace | Jealousy |
| Patience | Fits of Rage |
| Kindness | Selfishness |
| Goodness | Dissension |
| Faithfulness | Envy |
| Self-Control | Ambivalence |

My beliefs must be evident in the way I speak and behave toward others. It's a never-ending spiritual QA process. It's a cycle of continuous improvement in which the Holy Spirit and I evaluate my words and actions against God's behavioral criteria.

Many clients I have coached over the years have quietly thanked me and stated that I helped them beyond being better at customer service. They share that the principles and service skills I taught them helped them to be a better person. I couldn't ask for a higher compliment.

My face won't grace a magazine cover, but I've helped a fellow human being be a better person. I am so good with that.

## *"Not Applicable" Is Definitely Applicable*

But what happens if the customer's name was never provided in the call? Or what happens if the customer hung up before the rep could say goodbye?

*Not applicable* is an important consideration in evaluating customer interactions. Remember the audit where we discovered the tech support manager scored falsely to ensure his bonus? His team's inflated scores were not completely his fault. It's time now to discuss the flaws in our client's internal QA method. The client fell prey to a common methodology mistake that skews outcomes and introduces data noise. Their internal scorecard made no allowances for criteria that did not apply in a call.

If a criterion didn't apply, the default answer was *Yes*, as if it applied and the CSR demonstrated the behavior. The supervisor may have scored dishonestly by giving credit for things his team members missed. The team's QA methods compounded the problem.

Let's say that there were twenty behaviors on the scorecard and the TSR missed two of them. That's an outcome of 90%. But what if ten of the twenty behaviors weren't applicable in the call? The reality is that the TSR only demonstrated eight of the ten applicable behaviors, which is only 80%. It appears the TSR performed better because the system credits the TSR for ten behaviors that weren't relevant.

My client said he had suspicions about the QA reports he got from his internal team. Our audit revealed he was skeptical with good reason. He received QA reports full of inflated, misleading data. If you can game the system to skew the outcomes, then the outcomes can't be trusted. The outcome of any good QA process is a consistently excellent customer experience. That's the only outcome that matters to your customer.

## An Outcome Reflective of the Customer

I have a gaming system in our family room. I'm not a hardcore gamer, but I grew up with the advent of video games and video game consoles. I was a kid when the first Pong video games appeared next to pinball machines at the bowling alley. My inner child is thrilled to get lost in a game more real than my ten-year-old self rotating the Pong paddle could have imagined.

This leads me to another confession. I love making a PlayStation baseball player with my name and boosting the ratings so my video likeness becomes the greatest player ever. I'll play an entire season, hit eighty home runs with my .500 batting average before the All-Star break. Then, I'll crush it in the Home Run Derby on my way to a record-breaking triple-crown.

It's fun for my inner child. I played only two years of Little League as a kid. In those two years I got one hit, about which I recall every detail. I rode the bench more than I played the field. In Pee Wee League, this is a leading indicator of zero athletic ability.

Our client with the inflated scores is no different from me gigging my PlayStation to produce superhuman outcomes. I know the numbers aren't real, but too many QA programs pretend their reports are.

So what is the right way to build a QA scorecard?

Start with the Holy Trinity of CSAT as a foundation. Then, build a solid framework of customer-focused behavioral criteria. QA results will then reflect how a typical customer would rate each experience.

Our methodology uses a 100-point scale that considers only applicable behaviors in the calculation. We customize each scorecard based on the client's customers and the team's call flow. Once we have our behavioral criteria set, we combine them into categories. For simplicity, let's say that we use the Holy Trinity of CSAT as a guide. We put all the behaviors that impact resolution into one category. The second category consists of behaviors related to courtesy and friendliness. Time-related dimensions of service make up the third category.

Our research tells us what percentage of each of those pieces of the satisfaction pie drives the customer's overall satisfaction. Let's say it's 60 percent resolution, 25 percent courtesy and friendliness, and 15 percent time-related dimensions of service. When calculating an OSI, we weight the categories to reflect how your customer thinks. A CSR's

OSI for a call drops most when they miss a resolution-related behavior because customers penalize that the most.

During the creation of a scorecard for a client, I test the scorecard by considering whether the OSI from a sample of calls reflects satisfaction. When we do a pilot SQA for a client, the average OSI tends to land between the mid-seventies and mid-eighties.

The most exceptional teams I've ever worked with produce OSI average scores between ninety-five and ninety-eight. It takes time and effort to get there. It's easy for most teams to improve their OSI from eighty to ninety. They simply address low-hanging fruit and increase the demonstration of a few simple service skills. Getting a team from ninety to ninety-five is much harder. It begins to require behavior modification, and many people don't want to change. Getting a team consistently above ninety-five usually requires a combination of vision, culture, expectations, buy-in, accountability, and incentives.

When clients use our cycle of continuous improvement, the results become self-evident in our customer surveys. Customer satisfaction climbs alongside ratings for future purchase intent and likelihood to recommend. Sales also increase with improved customer loyalty and retention.

Why wouldn't any business want the benefits and positive outcomes of a continuous improvement model and robust QA process? Everyone wants the results. But common obstacles keep many businesses from making the investment.

Even the best-designed frameworks run headlong into a stubborn reality: People don't always want to change. It's the most common roadblock I've observed. It reveals itself in various "Yeah, but . . ." sentiments mentioned earlier. Let's explore a few of the most common.

## "Yeah, But . . ." Time

Time-related dimensions of service have become increasing drivers of customer satisfaction. But customers aren't the only ones feeling the increasing pressures of time. It's driving team members' perceptions as well.

"Yeah, but Tom, all these customer service skills add time to a customer conversation. I don't have time to say all these things."

I get this one from CSRs a lot. It might seem logical that asking associates to include certain words or phrases in a call will only increase the length of that call. It's not. Whenever I'm confronted with this argument, I offer an experiment. I suggest we "go to the tape" and let the data prove whether they are right or wrong.

The length of the call is a common QA metric. As I mentioned earlier, call length is not itself a measure of quality, but it can be a friend. To address the time concern, I pull a large sample of calls that had an OSI of 100. Every service criterion was met. Then, I calculate the average call time of these calls. I'll do the same thing with an equally large sample calls that scored below eighty-five.

If my client is right, calls that scored 100 should have much higher average lengths than those in which the CSRs did not include many of the behavioral elements. Not once has this proven true. In fact, it's common to find the calls that scored one hundred to be shorter on average. Why? Because great service focuses on quickly moving a customer toward a resolution in a courteous and friendly way. Those who excel at doing so become better and better at doing it efficiently and effectively.

## "Yeah, but . . ." Cost

A recurring roadblock I encounter from the C-suite is the cost-center mentality.

We were once hired by a client after a national survey ranked their operation's customer satisfaction among the lowest in the country. A middle manager, tasked with moving the needle, convinced her superiors to invest in Intelligentics for a company-wide event to kick-start a positive internal change.

I have visited many gorgeous corporate facilities, but even I was immediately impressed with this client's operation. They obviously spared no expense in their physical footprint. Everything was downright luxurious. The executive suite was palatial. There was even a game room filled with high-end games and gadgets that Big Tech firms like Google made the world think were essential to team morale.

The event went well, but the problem with one-time events is that they don't really do much to guarantee lasting success. If beautiful weddings guaranteed a happy marriage, there would be fewer divorces. After the event, as we discussed what it takes to measure and improve actual behavior, the client's defensive walls went up.

"Yeah, but Tom? How much is this going to cost?"

Every project we create for a client can be customized. Our clients have an entire team of research and QA experts implementing a model of continuous improvement and moving the needle on customer satisfaction, retention, and loyalty for less than the total cost of one full-time employee, and there are no strings attached. The question is what the client truly values.

One day I was talking with the executive president of one of our largest and most loyal clients.

"Vander Well? Do you know why I keep you guys around?" he asked me.

"Why is that?"

"Because I can pick up a phone and fire you whenever I want," he answered with a chuckle.

"Excuse me?"

"You guys are great at what you do. If I had to try to do all these surveys and do QA internally, I'd have to hire an entire team of people. There's no way I could hire your level of experience or expertise. I'd have to hire inexperienced people who don't know what they're doing. The results would be terrible. But then I'm stuck with all these costly employees. It would cost way more in the long run. I love knowing that I can pick up the phone at any moment and fire you. I sleep better at night knowing that."

My client had done the math. He found that what we provided for his company was profitable, and he recognized that having us do it was of greater value than just the expense of the annual contract.

We live in a DIY culture. Big Tech wants everyone to believe that they have the software to do everything yourself and that it will be cheaper, faster, and easier. Sometimes it's true. Sometimes it's an illusion that has made Big Tech companies a lot of money without ever delivering on their promises.

## "Yeah, but . . ." AI

I've observed that Big Tech is the tail that wags the dog in business. Each year at large industry trade shows, the focus is on what technology is the new must-have solution. Executives line up to get the latest and greatest. There is peer pressure in this. I've seen it in C-suite colleagues. Executives want to appear that they are on the cutting edge. They don't want to be the one who missed the bus. The IT team keeps a list of must-haves, and no one wants to get left behind. Tech is the bandwagon, and executives jump on board.

Sometimes the latest fad is truly a game changer. Other times it's a bust.

Big Tech and telephony companies have been selling AI-driven QA solutions for some time. In recent years, we've had two clients who made costly investments in a QA software solution rather than renewing their contract with Intelligentics. In both cases, I followed up with the client a year later to ask how the AI software was working. In both cases, the client had abandoned it for the same three reasons.

First, it took far more time and work than expected. AI had to be programmed to learn what to listen for, monitored to make sure it was catching the right things, and tweaked constantly. QA team members were sold on technology that would save them time. The promise was that they'd be freed up to do more coaching and training. The reality was that they spent more time trying to make AI work and never realized the benefits on which they'd been sold.

I attended a professional roundtable at which companies using AI software swapped best practices. The companies were unanimous in explaining that it required far more work hours to utilize the software than they expected. One expert suggested that those implementing a software-based QA solution should plan on adding at least five full-time employees to set it up, manage it, and keep it updated. Even then, the results are not always accurate.

Second, AI consistently analyzed calls incorrectly. One client told me about the multitude of calls the software flagged to be reviewed by a human. AI reported that the customer was highly escalated. "Not once was it correct," my former client laughed. "I wasted so much time on wild goose chases."

Both clients spoke of the lack of confidence AI software created across the operation. Front-line agents learned they couldn't trust it to be consistently correct. The QA team and the managers responsible for the technology got tired of fighting with it. They became even more drained trying to shore up morale around the supposed solution.

Third, current technology does not yet efficiently and cost-effectively analyze a conversation in larger business contexts. Each conversation is only a fraction of the customer's journey. Many factors outside of a single customer interaction impact the interaction and the outcome. The customer has to find a phone number, navigate the VRU, and get to the right department. Internal conflicts between teams can leave customers trapped. Quality analysis also depends on the CSR's attitude and performance history. Technology glitches and information access also play a role. All these nuances drive satisfaction for every company's customer base. An effective and cost-effective AI solution has yet to navigate these nuances in a solution that is accessible and affordable to most businesses.

Technology continues to advance. The efficiency and cost-effectiveness of AI will improve. AI will play a larger role in measuring service quality. Our clients spent far more money on Big Tech's promises than they were paying Intelligentics. They were sold on the promise of long-term time and cost savings. Within a year, both clients tossed the QA technology in the closet next to the box of Palm Pilots.

When done right, human beings are still an economical and efficient QA solution for most businesses.

## Beyond the CSR: The Benefits of Human Analysis

We were doing a pilot SQA for a new client, a family-owned business that provided in-home services. The owner was acquiring smaller businesses in the area to grow the company's footprint and customer base. After the merger, the owner observed cultural differences between the core business and the businesses they'd acquired. They wondered if these differences diluted the customer experience.

We discovered what I expected: the core sales and support team was good, but there was opportunity. The low-hanging fruit for quick improvement was ripe on the vine. But there were opportunities for improvement that had nothing to do with what the agents said or how they said it. They were rooted in basic operations.

- A CSR told a new customer their contract would be delivered by the USPS to sign and mail back. Hello, twenty-first century! Why would any company use such an archaic process riddled with delays and opportunities just to lose the sale altogether?

- There were no security protocols for customers and their accounts. Customers weren't being verified consistently. Anyone could call and get secure information or place orders without question.

- The sales team defaulted to offering customers the lowest-cost options. Their intent was to save the customers money. But this approach ensured lower revenues, and unnecessary contacts from unhappy customers.

- There were multiple instances of single-point failures. For example, instead of handling a caller's concern, customers had to wait for a call back from the same rep they talked to last time.

- Teams were structured in such a way that even new customers were constantly getting bounced back and forth between teams. The process was inefficient, and it aggravated customers.

- The business owner's suspicions also proved true. Through technology, the teams from the acquired companies were merged into one virtual team. However, because the teams remained separate physically, they didn't feel like they were part of the new company. Some of the team members refused to adopt the new procedures. They complained about the new owners and the transition to existing customers. They were resistant to change.

It is easy for executives to think QA is about holding CSRs accountable to a process. That is the core motivation for doing QA. However, there is so much more to learn from analyzing your customers' experience.

Our monthly SQA reports to clients include a section of observations, questions, and suggestions for the management team. We raise issues like the examples I've just listed. Beyond the CSRs' service skills, there are policies, procedures, and systems that work against both the customer and the company. Every company has a host of blind spots. They are on full display during customer interactions, but most companies don't look for them. Most internal QA programs don't look for them. Yet QA can be a revealing spotlight that asks, "Why on earth are we doing it this way?"

I've provided QA for a veritable plethora of companies. With that experience comes knowledge of countless unique challenges. I've learned what works and what doesn't. When I analyze calls, I bring all of that knowledge and experience with me into the analysis. I bring knowledge of systemic best practices as well as urban myths of business that drive poor decisions and procedures. I'm not just a mechanical translator programmed to determine whether certain words or voice tones were present. I'm constantly looking at the larger customer journey and service delivery system. I will address the CSRs with opportunities they have to improve each customer interaction. I will also address management with the opportunities they have to improve their policies, procedures, and systems. A culture of service excellence requires both. Once again, I find myself a man in the middle.

## The Man in the Middle Between the Front Line and the C-Suite

I was between training sessions at a client contact center. We had been working with this client for about a year, and I had gotten to know some of the CSRs, including a retired gentleman working to supplement his income. He had spent a lifetime in business and had a lot to offer. He did a nice job on the phone. He also had the wisdom and experience to see what needed improvement.

One day, he stopped me in the hallway and said, "I just wanted to say thank you. Since your team has been working with the company, I've seen so many positive changes. You know what? So many of them are things that we've suggested or complained about for years, but nobody ever listens to us. They are listening to you, and I really, really appreciate it. Keep up the good work. You're making a positive difference!"

I've gotten compliments like that a lot in my career because of a common dilemma in business. I find layers of bureaucracy between the CSRs and the C-suite. It silences the voices of those most familiar with customer pain points. Executives get shielded from problems and are told what they want to hear.

I love metaphors because they contain multiple layers of meaning. I shared that being the man in the middle means being a spiritually motivated person working in the business world. The same metaphor has other layers of meaning. It's about holding the tension between Cheerleader and the Heated Blacksmith. It's also about bridging the gap between front-line CSRs and executives. The agents in the trenches need an advocate whom management will listen to. Executives need an ally who will tell them the truths that their team may be hiding. Our method of continuous improvement allows me to do both. It's been one of the most rewarding aspects of my career.

It's such a blessing to work with individuals throughout their careers. I've walked alongside new employees and coached them as they rose in the ranks. I've accompanied executives in their first major role in a corporation. This is where the Blacksmith traits of the job give way to the Cheerleader in my soul. I get to be a morale booster and a motivator. I love it.

# CHAPTER 5

# Motivation and Morale

We had the privilege of helping one client build the strongest service quality culture I've ever seen. It began with a few teams in one department. We saw measurable improvement through our three-step continuous improvement model. Service quality improved, customer satisfaction rose, and the company's profits grew. Our SQA expanded across other departments and their teams.

The client was part of a much larger global corporation. As they became among the most profitable subsidiaries in the portfolio, they drew increased attention from corporate leadership. That's when things began to shift—but not for the better.

Our continuous improvement model is built on a simple but powerful premise: set a high standard that exceeds customer expectations. Then, monitor customer feedback through research, assess service delivery through SQA, and coach your team toward consistent excellence. When the bar needs to be raised, raise it.

To illustrate, let's go back to our metaphor from professional football. Offensive and defensive linemen spend every day practicing the fundamentals. The boring elements of blocking and tackling are the foundation of champions. After each game, they review the tape, dissect every movement, and look for ways to improve. Even the best players continue improving because trophies are won and lost in one missed play. One missed tackle or one missed block can be the difference between a win and a loss. The pursuit of excellence never stops.

We set the bar high with our SQA. A perfect SQA score is the exception, not the rule. I've seen only two individuals maintain a 100-point average for an entire quarter. Many consistently score in the upper nineties, but even that takes focus, discipline, and effort. Continuous improvement requires that you're always reaching for better. You're only reaching for better if the bar is set just beyond your grasp.

As our long-term client attracted attention from corporate leadership, a competing philosophy emerged. It came from the executive Cheerleaders. With good intent, they wanted to boost confidence and foster a positive environment. This created a shift.

The shift was from a customer-centered model to an employee-centered one. It came at a cost. It's easy for most associates to score 100 consistently. You simply lower the bar. The predictable result is mediocrity. Customer satisfaction erodes. And ironically, the morale boost they hoped to achieve often proves fleeting.

In contrast, I've seen what happens when teams reach for excellence. They take pride in the experience they deliver. They notice how other companies fall short on the basics. They become mentors to new colleagues, modeling the standard. And yes, they sometimes struggle with teammates who resist the higher bar, but they keep going.

There's a deep sense of satisfaction when you have the data to prove how hard you worked to reach the top of your game. It feels good to know you made a difference.

Sadly, our relationship with the client who embraced the esteem-first approach came to an end. We insisted that their brand of world-class excellence required nothing less than a commensurate high standard. They insisted that a lower standard of excellence that team members could consistently reach without effort was important. The shift in philosophy made it impossible to continue the work we'd started.

My insistence on setting a high standard is, in part, based on solid business practices of companies that have succeeded through delivering on a brand promise of service excellence. It is also rooted in my spiritual formation experience.

# Life Lesson: The Jesus Paradigm of Transformation

*Do nothing out of selfish ambition or vain conceit.
Rather, in humility value others above yourselves,
not looking to your own interests but each of you to
the interests of the others.*
Philippians 2:3-4

In your relationships with one another, have the same
mindset as Christ Jesus:

*Who, being in very nature God,
  did not consider equality with God something to
be used to his own advantage;
rather, he made himself nothing
  by taking the very nature of a servant,
  being made in human likeness.
And being found in appearance as a man,
  he humbled himself
  by becoming obedient to death—
    even death on a cross!*
Philippians 2:6-11

*From that time on Jesus began to preach, "Repent,
for the kingdom of heaven has come near."*
Matthew 4:17

Things immediately changed the night I gave my life
to Jesus. A year earlier, I was a depressed teenager

filled with self-doubt. I entertained suicidal thoughts. Suddenly, I was a young man on a mission, filled with a desire to make a difference in my world.

How did Jesus motivate this change in me?

First, He focused not on Himself and His place on an eternal throne, but rather focused on us—on me. He left His throne and emptied Himself. He came to earth to be one of us, to live with us, to love us, and even to die for us.

Second, He called me to change. The word *repent* means to turn around and go in the opposite direction. Jesus loved me in all my self-centeredness, my teen angst, and my depression. At the same time, He called me to live differently. He knew there was so much more for me, but it required an inner transformation.

Third, He slowly changed me to follow the imprint of His sandals from the throne room to the cross. Jesus's love was all about me so that my life and love could be all about others.

I have been walking in the steps of those sandals for well over forty years. The cycle of repentance, change, and living for others never ends. I'm still learning things about myself that need to change. It took fifty years to realize what an envious person I am. That needed to change. I'm still pressing myself to love others in higher, deeper, and broader ways.

I return to God's QA criteria for life every day:

Love
Joy
Peace
Patience
Kindness
Goodness
Faithfulness
Self-Control

I never score 100. But Jesus calls me to wake-up every morning, keep changing, and continue improving. The better I get at it, the more fulfilled I am in life, in relationships, and in my own being.

I believe that Jesus's pedagogy is the best template for helping my clients succeed and find satisfaction in a job well done. It is a journey both in life and in business.

## The Service Excellence Journey

No matter the size or shape of the company, the continuous improvement process follows a well-beaten path. At Intelligentics, we call our continuous improvement method the *Service Excellence Journey.*

The first phase of the Service Excellence Journey is applied knowledge. The first step exposes ignorance. We don't know what we don't know. We begin by uncovering blind spots through customer research and the initial SQA pilot assessment. Revealing customer expectations and current service levels provides the roadmap for improvement and the route we need to take.

The second phase addresses individual performance gaps. Insights spark growth, but to move forward, everyone must understand their role. Every team member needs to contribute. As long as there are stragglers refusing to come along, the Promised Land of service excellence remains out of reach.

The third and longest phase I call the *Long Slog*. This is the wilderness where everyone learns to work together, stay aligned, and gut it out through consistent change and adaptation. The Long Slog requires faith and perseverance.

Last is the coveted customer-service Promised Land. With sustained effort, an organization will reach a point where excellence consistently hums in every customer experience and continuous improvement becomes the norm.

Let's take a closer look at each phase of the journey.

## Phase 1: Applied Knowledge

If you want to improve your health, the first thing that a doctor or physical therapist will do is a thorough assessment. Tests identify strengths and needs. The resulting intelligence is translated into tactics. A regimen of diet, exercise, and supplements is prescribed. If followed, a patient's health efficiently improves.

This same paradigm is true of business health. Teams are stuck in the chains of mediocrity the same way an individual gets stuck in unhealthy life patterns. Getting unstuck requires the same intelligence translated into prescribed tactics. This is what Intelligentics' pilot project accomplishes. In sixty to ninety days, we walk a new client through our three-step continuous improvement model: customer survey, SQA, and a team training event. The method jump-starts the Service Excellence Journey through actionable insight.

Understanding what your customers think and expect provides both motivation and direction. Most team members want to do a good job. They genuinely desire to provide a great customer experience, but that experience has never been clearly defined for them. And if it has, it likely hasn't come from the actual customers they interact with every day. There is power in revealing the results of a survey that shows where customers see room for improvement. I often enhance the data with video-taped and edited interviews to give a face and a voice to the data. There is a powerful epiphany when team members hear a real customer express dissatisfaction or desire.

Knowing how the team is performing provides clarity. Customer research gives us the destination. SQA data provides a roadmap for resolving customer dissatisfaction. The data helps us understand if the caller got the run-around, their questions weren't answered, or they weren't treated well. The SQA pinpoints where the team is missing opportunities to deliver what its customers desire. The SQA also provides a balanced report with both service skills and policy or procedural issues. Front-line team members are encouraged to see that the critique isn't just about their behavior. It's also about the systemic issues that frustrate them every day.

Prioritized training that offers simple tactics and techniques empowers immediate change. In most cases, a long list of improvement opportunities surfaces through the pilot SQA. The improvement journey gets off to a fast start when we target the low-hanging fruit that will have maximum impact. Data from the customer survey tells us what drives customer satisfaction. We can prioritize training on the skills that will have the quickest and most significant impact on customer satisfaction.

Phase 1 is focused on the team. It's about giving them knowledge of customer expectations, an accurate assessment of service levels, and practical ways to improve. As I mentioned earlier, it's common for teams to begin the journey with an OSI in the upper seventies to mid-eighties on a 100-point scale. Within a year, most teams improve to the low nineties.

That's where things stall.

## Phase 2: The Individual Performance Gap

Let's continue considering the parallel paradigm of personal health improvement. If you have ever made long-term efforts at weight loss and improved health, you know that improvement doesn't follow a smooth and consistent pattern. A quick loss in weight might be followed by a long set-point in which nothing changes for a long time despite faithfully following the prescribed regimen.

For clients on the Service Excellence Journey, an inevitable stall in improvement happens after relatively rapid success. Every team has a spectrum of performance, so let's return to our bell curve. At one end of the bell curve are the perfectionists and go-getters. They have applied the knowledge and motivated themselves toward service excellence. They have driven the team's improvements. These team members often have individual OSI averages above 95. At the other end of the bell curve are team members plagued by any number of symptoms that keep them from performing to their capability. They might be resistant to change. They might have a bad attitude. They might simply be passive. Whatever the issue, they're not improving. In the middle of the bell curve sits the majority of the team. They made a few simple and positive changes that contributed to the initial improvement. They haven't, however, employed all the service skills. They aren't working on skills that require effort and habit change. If they don't, the team will never reach the customer-experience Promised Land.

In Phase 2, the shift from a team-based approach to an individual-based approach is required. Every individual receives detailed monthly performance feedback. Management gets the data as well. Individual results enable the crucial conversations needed for renewed momentum.

The move to individual focus boosts morale among higher performers. Their strong performance is documented. That top performance can be recognized and rewarded by management. Top performers are also encouraged that lower-performing team members are being held accountable. Managers can have crucial conversations, increase coaching, and provide accountability for team members whose service performance hasn't improved. If low performers and stuck performers don't begin to improve, the team will never reach its goal. It's time to start motivating behavioral change. This leads to the next phase of the journey. It's the phase I call the Long Slog.

## Phase 3: The Long Slog

Bilbo had Mirkwood. Harry Potter and his friends had the Forbidden Forest. Luke Skywalker had Dagobah. Every epic journey includes a wilderness experience in which the hero must learn hard lessons that are only possible in the struggle. The journey to service excellence is no different.

Our team has been walking through the Long Slog with one client for several years. They've made great progress, but there's an outlier. There's a legacy CSR with a refusal to change. Management's approach to this individual has been to placate him until he retired. In the meantime, God help any customer who has the misfortune of reaching that team member when they call.

This is a textbook example of what contributes to the Long Slog. Consistent service excellence requires more than the front-line agents. It requires corporate vision and commitment at all levels from all teams. The team will never be consistently excellent with a toxic team member answering calls every day. Management can hold the team member accountable, move them to a non-customer-facing position, dismiss them, or do nothing. In this case, they chose to do nothing until the problem naturally went away.

The Long Slog continues for a host of reasons. One client had a great customer support team. However, the customer experience regularly hinged on the accounting team. This team refused to speak with customers. They failed to resolve customer problems in an efficient manner. They wouldn't reply to customer support team members. The accounting team's manager refused to address the issues.

Service excellence and continuous improvement require that all teams are aligned and focused. This includes teams that aren't customer-facing but still impact the customer experience. Systemic issues must be addressed. Technology must be upgraded.

Changing a company culture from service mediocrity to service excellence requires persistence and perseverance. But it can be done, and it's worth the slog. I've seen the rewards when clients finally reach the Promised Land.

## Phase 4: The Promised Land

During the Long Slog, I've observed that certain things begin to happen and fall into place. The employee who refuses to change retires. Those who thought this would be just another fad realize they have to get on board. New associates embrace the service quality expectations and skills required from day one. Rising customer satisfaction and quality scores become a matter of pride. Good performance is spotlighted and rewarded. What was once a new and uncomfortable call for change becomes the norm. The entire operation is tooled to deliver consistently. Service excellence is now part of the culture.

It's great to reach a place where service excellence and high levels of customer satisfaction are expected. I love hearing team members tell new employees, "This is just how we do things. We take pride in delivering an exceptional customer experience."

It's important to realize, however, that the journey never really ends.

Let's return to professional sports as an example. Athletes get larger, faster, and stronger. Records continue to fall, the sport evolves, and the standard of excellence continues to rise along with expectations.

It is no different with business. Technology has changed the way we think and behave, and the customer experience we expect. In recent years, our team has seen what we call the *Amazon Effect* on customer expectations in B2B industries. Consumers have become so used to items being in stock, same-day delivery, and endless streams of communication telling them where their package is, if it's delayed, and when it's delivered. They are increasingly demanding the same experience from every vendor they order from at work. B2B companies are seeing lower customer satisfaction and higher customer expectations.

Generational differences are currently also wreaking havoc in certain customer populations. The differences in expectations between Generations X, Y, and Z are stark. To adapt and survive, businesses must pivot everything from marketing to customer support. Different generations have different expectations for communication, resolution, and time-related dimensions of service. These generational shifts are creating new internal challenges in maintaining service excellence.

No business reaches a point at which the continuous improvement cycle is no longer relevant. Keep your finger on the pulse of shifting customer expectations. Keep your eyes and ears on your team's service quality. Keep coaching and training to meet and exceed customer expectations. The journey never ends.

## Life Lesson: The Exodus Paradigm

All epic stories contain wilderness experiences. The Service Excellence Journey I just described has its own Long Slog. The journey of Moses and the tribes of Israel from Egypt to the Promised Land is primary source material. There are three key phases in that particular journey. I call it the *Exodus Paradigm.*

The road out of slavery in Egypt.

The road through the wilderness.

The road into the Promised Land.

This paradigm is repeated over and over throughout the Great Story. You'll find it in the Psalms, the prophets, and in the exiles of Israel. Jesus begins His three-year ministry as He rises from His baptism and out of His former life. Then, He enters the wilderness where He is tempted before emerging into the ministry for which He came.

The Exodus Paradigm is also referenced in the New Testament. Every believer's journey is a retelling of the Exodus Paradigm. We are led by God's Spirit out of our slavery to sin. We are led through the wilderness of this fallen world, in which every trial matures us toward completion. One day, we will cross the heavenly Jordan River and enter eternity's Promised Land.

My career has been a consistent reminder of the journey we all walk. I lead and accompany clients on their journeys toward excellence. I do the same for individual team members. All the while I've been on my own journey.

The Exodus Paradigm repeats itself in every area and season of life.

Each phase of the journey is spiritually important. The long, challenging stretches are the most important, even as I grumble about the conditions and duration. I develop faith, patience, perseverance, maturity, and hope only through the wilderness and monotony of the Long Slog.

In every phase of the journey, I have learned to rest in the knowledge that I am being led. I can trust the Lord whose sandal prints I'm following. Even He had His "I'm not sure about this" moment in the Garden of Gethsemane.

Even He had to find His "not My will, but Yours" faith. Even He had to walk the path of suffering and death to arrive at the Promised Land of Resurrection.

This is the way. I can have an attitude of bitterness, resentment, and resistance, or I can have an attitude of faith, trust, and hope.

That choice is perpetually mine every step of the journey.

Along my career journey, I came to realize that my team could produce more data than the client could absorb. But data alone never transforms a culture. For that, something deeper must change, something human.

## Attitude

Jerry was a senior member of a team that handled large credit decisions for a major financial institution. We'd been working with his team for about fifteen years. Jerry was always good-natured during coaching sessions; however, his SQA scores remained just so-so. He had a natural charisma, so I knew he could do a much better job on the phone.

Then came one random month in which I noticed Jerry was doing everything I'd been coaching him to do for many years. He was courteous and personable. He apologized for the unmet expectations. He even confirmed that the customer had no further questions or issues before closing the call. That month, he was the highest performer on the team.

The next time I was in Jerry's building, I looked him up.

"Great job, Jerry!" I said, giving him a high-five. "You've been doing great!"

He laughed and nodded his head wordlessly.

"What made the change?" I asked.

"When you guys started this whole service quality thing, I figured it was just another short-lived management initiative. I decided right away that you couldn't make me change. I was determined to wait it out. One day I realized that you hadn't gone away and there's really no reason for me not to do the things you've taught me. It's not hard."

He shrugged.

"I just decided it was time for me to do it."

Jerry remained a top performer throughout the rest of his career. He represents the greatest challenge I encounter with every client: attitude. All kinds of attitudes become obstacles to change and improvement.

Stan was a very large man. He was also a very angry man, and my coaching became one of his triggers. In my entire career, coaching Stan was the only time I felt physically threatened. I'm happy to report that my fears were never realized.

Lynn was defiant. She crossed her arms and stared at the floor when I'd present at team meetings. She refused to make eye contact or acknowledge me no matter how friendly I was. In our coaching sessions, she would turn her chair to face the wall. She kept her back to me the entire session. She gave me the silent treatment.

Tanisha was one of the nicest people I ever met. We got along great. She was a pleasant avoider. She came into every coaching session with a larger-than-life smile. She wanted to know everything about me and my family. She would talk my arm off and charm the heck out of me. She also wanted nothing to do with listening to her calls or changing what she said in customer interactions. She leveraged her energy and charisma to turn our session into a social hour. Anything to avoid being coached or having to change.

I quickly learned in my career that I was working with people who have different histories, temperaments, and motivations. There is no one-size-fits-all approach to motivating and coaching them to change and improve. To succeed, I would have to change my coaching approach depending on the person I was coaching.

## Motivation and the Nine Types

Do you remember the young salesman who began our first call-coaching session with his expletive-laden tirade? His attitude toward me and the process didn't change the fact that I had to coach him every quarter. As I got to know him, it was obvious that he was driven. He attacked his sales job with passion. Why? He loved money. He wanted to make more money so he could fulfill all his material desires.

After meditating on this, I began our next coaching meeting appealing to his motivation. I told him, "I know you think all this is QA and call coaching is silly and you're only here because you have to be, but please hear me out. The things I'm trying to coach you to do are based on what we know drives your customers' satisfaction. There's not one service skill I'm trying to teach you that won't be appreciated and make them more satisfied. The customer who loves how you care for them is more likely to give you their business. You make more money."

Bingo.

His attitude toward me didn't change much, but the data from his calls showed that he slowly incorporated the things I taught him. He became even more successful and rose in the ranks of the client's sales organization.

I learned that to be a successful coach, I had to study people to learn what motivates them. I returned to my actor's training in which great performances begin with understanding your character's motivation.

There are many assessments and personality tests utilized by businesses. I've taken and utilized Myers-Briggs, DiSC, and many others over the years. Then I discovered the Enneagram and eventually became certified as a coach. I love the Enneagram. Instead of placing people in four quadrants, the Enneagram identifies nine different types, each with its own core strengths, fears, and motivations. It also details unique complexities within each type. I'm a Type 4, the Individualist. I'm also a countertype—someone who doesn't exhibit all the classic marks of a Type 4 on the surface.

Each of the nine types exhibits certain conflict styles, coping styles, and communication styles. As I coach people, I've learned to identify what those are. I can tailor my coaching to be more analytical, motivational, or inspirational depending on who I'm working with. Some individuals simply need me to give them the information straight. Other individuals need me to earn their trust and know I care about them. To help people improve the customer experience, I have to understand who they are and how to communicate with them effectively.

## Life Lesson: Setting People Up to Succeed

*Now if the foot should say, "Because I am not a hand, I do not belong to the body," it would not for that reason stop being part of the body. And if the ear should say, "Because I am not an eye, I do not belong to the body," it would not for that reason stop being part of the body. If the whole body were an eye, where would the sense of hearing be? If the whole body were an ear, where would the sense of smell be? But in fact, God placed the parts in the body, every one of them, just as he wanted them to be. If they were all one part, where would the body be? As it is, there are many parts, but one body.*
1 Corinthians 12:15–19

A senior manager asked for advice about a long-time team member's possible promotion. I'd been working with his team for over a decade. Despite making some improvements, the team member had always been a low performer. They posted for a promotion to a position the senior manager knew wasn't a good fit. However, he was pressured. Moving a tenured employee up the ladder seemed like the right thing to do.

We had a very good conversation about setting people up for success. Not only was the team member a mismatch for the open position, but our SQA data showed he wasn't a great fit for the role they'd been in for years. This individual was very smart and capable, but they weren't a great communicator. The team member was unhappy in their job, and they treated customers accordingly. The team member needed a back-office position in which their knowledge and experience would help them excel and the need for interpersonal communication was minimized.

When I was on my personal path toward pastoral ministry, I observed something that consistently created problems for the churches I attended and served. Individuals desired to be in positions for which they were ill-suited. The lady who couldn't carry a tune wanted to sing in the spotlight. The worship guy thought himself a preacher and gave a mini-sermon between every song. Even educational institutions cranked out pastors who were awful preachers and even worse leaders. Having the credential doesn't mean you have the gift.

I have found Paul's simple metaphor about the body to be apt well beyond the paradigm of the church. It's relevant to every business, organization, and human system. For the whole to function well, individuals within that system need to understand their gifts, abilities, and bents. Desiring a position doesn't mean you're good at it, nor will your desire translate into what's best for the whole.

All of us are gifted in some areas, functional in other areas, and ill-suited for other roles.

I love music. I wish I were a gifted singer and musician, but I'm not. I am functional. Our church had no bass player, but there was an electric bass sitting on the platform during worship. I asked our worship leader about it. She said that it belonged to the church, but no one played. I asked her if I could take it and play around with it. Over a couple of weeks, I taught myself how to plunk out a baseline and follow the chords. For a number of years, I became a regular bass player at multiple churches I attended. That said, I was functional at it. As soon as I found myself in a church with gifted musicians, I was quickly released from the worship team. I was fine with that. I had other, stronger gifts where the church had a need.

It is critical to the success of any system to have the right people in the right positions, where everyone functions within their strengths. When this happens, the whole organization benefits. When the wrong individuals are in the wrong roles, the pain of dysfunction resonates throughout the entire system.

Even when the system is healthy, individuals need to be motivated toward continuous improvement. In the process of leading improvement efforts for clients, I have learned a lot about how motivation works.

## The Carrot and the Stick

There are two primary forms of motivation and behavior reinforcement: positive and negative. I refer to them as the carrot and the stick. When our daughters were young, we did our best to use the carrot to get them to do their daily tasks and chores. We added gold stars to the chore charts on the fridge and gave other rewards and praise for completed tasks. We even paid out weekly allowances based on performance. We were always dangling the carrot of encouragement and reward in front of them to motivate positive behavior.

Then they became teenagers.

As normal teen attitudes set in, positive reinforcement ran out. The strategy quickly shifted toward constant reminders and negative consequences for non-adherence. We had to pull out the stick as threats to revoke privileges and garnish allowances.

I once thought that adulthood was the time when knowledge and maturity just sort of fell into place. Then I discovered that adults are basically children in bigger bodies. Even with the best of intentions, both the carrot and the stick are required for all ages.

Let's go back to the common phases of improvement I witness with clients on the journey to service excellence.

Phase 1: Applied Knowledge

Phase 2: Individual Performance Gap

Phase 3: The Long Slog

Phase 4: The Promised Land

Much like training children with their chores, the initial phase is all positive reinforcement. People don't know what they don't know, so we provide knowledge in a positive and encouraging way. We applaud behavior. In most cases, our clients don't even provide a tangible financial carrot in Phase 1. Improvement just happens.

Positive and negative reinforcement occur naturally in Phase 2. Strong performers are motivated by pride and public recognition. Lower performers get whacked with the shame of exposure. No longer able to hide behind team averages, lower performers have a choice. They can either end their pain and kick it into gear, or they can double-down on nonconformance and entrench their negative attitude.

In the Long Slog of Phase 3, clients introduce more tangible carrots and sticks into the process. No one likes to pull out the stick, so it starts with dangling carrots such as recognition, reward, and compensation. Gift cards, jeans day, and PTO are common carrots. Lunch with the boss is especially popular with larger companies in which employees might otherwise never meet the CEO. One client went for the big-ticket reward. Team members who scored 95 or higher each month in their SQA earned raffle tickets for a high-end lawn tractor worth thousands of dollars.

The stick comes out in tangible ways as well. Service quality scores factor into annual reviews, and poor results reduce or eliminate raises and bonuses.

The process itself continues to create its own carrots and sticks organically. During the Long Slog, top performers leverage their positive SQA scores when they apply and interview for promotions. Senior managers give preference to those who have proven to be self-motivated. In contrast, low performers discover that their low scores and reputations hinder their career goals and upward mobility. By Phase 4, the continuous improvement model is in full operation, and the carrots and sticks are in place.

Whether you're dealing with children or with adults, both positive and negative reinforcement are required. Once again, there is a tension in the wise application of both.

It begins with generous use of positive reinforcement and the sparing, judicious use of negative reinforcement only as required. The Cheerleaders of the world don't want to even consider the stick. The Blacksmiths can't wait to wield it. Wise leaders learn the tension and balance between the two. Just like the Hebrews needed Moses, wise leadership is crucial to the success of any service improvement journey.

# SECTION 3

# At the Top

# CHAPTER 6

# Leadership for the Service Excellence Journey

Company culture flows from the corner office of the C-suite. I've seen it again and again with clients, large and small. I once worked for a national retailer with a legacy of poor customer service. They made millions selling low-quality products to low-income customers. The secret to their profitability was closed-end credit. For example, they sold $30 bath towel sets on an easy installment plan of nine $5 payments.

The vice president of customer service set out to change the culture but first had to win over the executive team. He called us, and we proposed an aggressive, customized version of our continuous improvement model. The VP invited our leadership team to make the pitch to the company's executives and board.

"Great customer service?!" one board member exclaimed with incredulity after we finished our pitch. "We sell shit to nerds."

Wow! Talk about brand identity!

Through some sort of miracle, we got the green light, but the Long Slog began on day one. We stood against an entrenched legacy culture and an operational system built on disdain for its customers and minimizing the cost of serving them. It was almost as though someone told them they "sold shit to nerds."

## Servant Leadership

I learned many lessons on that project. The relationship lasted many years. The reason we had the opportunity and the company culture changed was the vision, leadership, and dogged determination of their vice president of customer service. He happened to be a sincere disciple of Jesus, and his faith motivated and informed everything he did.

The project was a master class in leadership at that early point in my career. He assembled a top-notch team of capable managers, mentored them, and inspired them to achieve amazing things. The VP served in humility. He taught his team to do the same as they served every low-income customer who wrote the CSRs' paychecks one threadbare towel at a time.

Our most successful client relationships have been with leaders who understand the profit in the Long Slog. They know that building and maintaining customer relationships pays off. During that legendary project, I saw the difference that one good leader can make in an otherwise unhealthy corporate system. The VP did it through consistent application of Jesus's Golden Rule. He applied it internally with his team, and then he motivated them to apply it with customers.

I've had the privilege of working with other amazing leaders whose examples I still follow. One CEO refused to work out of his corner office unless necessary for a private conversation. Instead, he worked in a cubicle outside the office on the open floor with the team. He wanted the team to see him working as hard as they did. He wanted the interactions that happened organically as people passed by. He wanted people to know that they could talk to him.

Another CEO made a point of casually walking through a different department of the company every day. He greeted team members by name and asked about their families and their lives. By example, he taught them to do the same with loyal customers on every call.

One successful business owner had a lavish lake home. She generously made it available for team members and their families to use rather than letting it sit empty.

I find that great CEOs and business owners seek candid feedback. They rarely get it from their own teams and direct reports who want to cover their rear ends and avoid uncomfortable conversations. Leadership shapes service excellence and a customer-focused culture for better or worse. Sometimes, it gets complicated. Leadership changes. Leadership that served a company for better, for a season, becomes leadership that stalls or diminishes success in the next season. When that happens, no one really wants to address the real issue.

## Gut Issues and Good People

Entrepreneurs are incredible people. I have so much respect for individuals who turn vision and passion into a successful business. As I've gotten to know these leaders and their businesses, I've noticed a few patterns.

Certain themes have emerged during introductory calls as potential clients share their stories. A visionary and passionate entrepreneur began the company. It became a great success. The founder remained on as CEO. It was evident that everyone in the organization revered them. Yet the company has hit a wall. Sales and growth curves once fit for a world-class mountain climber now resemble your average speed bump.

The founder usually digs their heels in first as we ask questions and discuss our continuous improvement method. Depending on their Enneagram type, they might vocalize their defensiveness or sit with crossed arms. The leadership team feels the pressure to get the company back into growth mode. The founder and CEO applies the pressure, but that same individual may be the most resistant. They don't want to admit what the data reveals or the level of help they need.

I've learned a lot about the circumstances that create this common scenario. The entrepreneurial founder started this business based on their gut instinct. They had a good gut. It proved correct. It led to great success. They've known loyal customers personally for years. Their gut has rarely, if ever, failed them. Until now. We have a leadership gut issue.

As businesses grow, the customer base grows with them. Eventually the customer base outgrows the founder's gut. It's impossible for any leader's gut to sense what an evolving customer base thinks and desires. Shifts in customer expectations based on technology or generational differences assure this. As we survey their customers, we discover the pain points that have reduced loyalty and retention and instigated customer churn. With it, we reveal the founder's blind spots. It's a humbling experience for someone with the visionary passion and hubris to build a successful business from nothing.

Entrepreneurial gut issues create symptoms beyond understanding customers and extend to the denial of what is happening on the team. Entrepreneurs are fiercely loyal to their team members because their team members have been fiercely loyal to them. The founder knows them, their spouses, and their families. In the founder's heart, their team is full of good people who fueled the success of their business. They are upstanding members of the community.

While that is true, good people don't always give great service. I've done a lot of SQA pilot assessments. I know that every team has a few good people who are not great communicators. SQA routinely reveals that most teams are balanced by customer service rock stars and those who would excel in a very different role. The majority of good people on the team fall somewhere in between. Their customer service skills are good. However, the reward for mediocre customer sales and support will never overcome the penalties of acute customer pain.

There are two keys to getting a stalled business back into growth mode. The first key is listening to customers, finding their pain points, and learning their expectations. The second key is measuring good reps, training them to excel, and giving them motivation and accountability to follow through.

Those things won't happen if a company's entrepreneurial founder is afraid to accept that the business has outgrown their gut. Fear short-circuits success in many ways.

## Scared Leadership

A long-term client was well into Phase 2 of the Service Excellence Journey. Excited with the results from the customer support team, the sales manager requested a pilot SQA for their sales team. Executive management agreed.

The company's financials were strong thanks in part to this sales team. Their customer base was growing, and the operation was expanding. The sales manager explained how the sales team was set up, the process they used, and what we could expect to hear in the phone calls. We randomly sampled a few hundred calls over a four-week period and quickly did the analysis.

Our analysis revealed something the sales manager didn't expect. All the outbound sales calls we'd been told the team was making every day didn't exist. Many customers called for quotes and orders. There was plenty of sales activity. However, each day the number of outbound sales and cold calls reported was grossly exaggerated at best.

I made a special trip to visit the sales manager and deliver the difficult news. I watched as he phased through the first few stages of grief until he got angry.

"My bosses can't see this report or know anything about what you've found," he told me emphatically.

I explained that he was the one who contracted the pilot assessment with us, not his bosses. Our obligation was to deliver the report to him. What he did with it was up to him. Then, I gave him some advice.

"The reason you do an SQA is to learn what is happening during customer interactions so you can improve—so you can hold your team accountable. I realize that this is embarrassing, but you didn't know what your team was doing. I know your bosses are people of integrity. I recommend an honest approach. Tell them the truth. Present a clear plan of action. Assure them the sales team will be stronger with ongoing assessment and accountability."

He buried the report. We never did another assessment for them. In less than a year, he left the company. I wish I could say this was the only time one of our projects was deep-sixed by a client. However, I'm happy to say it hasn't happened a lot. Every time it has happened, we were working with a manager other than the owner or CEO.

The data and recommendations in our reports allow clients to face the truth, make changes, hold team members accountable, and fix costly blind spots. It may be painful, but it's a blueprint for positive change and successful outcomes. Sometimes leaders are too paralyzed by the fear of perception. They are so afraid of looking bad that they ignore the results. They refuse to address the problems. It seems easier to shrug and keep doing things the way they've always been done.

If a team isn't doing well, the first question to ask is whether there is a leadership problem. That becomes difficult when the question must be asked in front of a mirror. As I said at the beginning of this section, a company's culture flows out of the corner office. The most toxic business environments I've ever encountered were rooted in toxic leadership.

## People, Not Pawns

The first time I walked into the client's contact center, it was a shock to my senses. It was in the basement of the client's corporate headquarters. It wasn't a contact center so much as a bunker. That's what our team began to call it. The rows of tiny agent stations were squeezed together to maximize headcount. Team members were packed in like sardines. I noticed hands in the air across the room as supervisors and managers scrambled from desk to desk addressing issues.

CSRs were tethered to their desks by policy. They were even forbidden to use the restroom without permission from a wandering supervisor. Lord, help the poor agent with a full bladder when all the supervisors were busy.

I've been blessed to work with clients who care about their customers and care about their team members. It's why they make the investment in Intelligentics and in the Service Excellence Journey. There is, however, another reality that exists in far too many businesses. It's what I experienced when I walked into the bunker. When executives value revenue more than people, their own team members become pawns in the pursuit of profit.

I entered the bunker because there was a new executive on the corporate team. She had turned a different retailer's corporate culture around. She learned her lessons well. She had been faithful with a few things. Now she was with a new employer and in charge of many things. That included turning their own corporate culture around. She called us, and we began the journey toward service excellence in the bunker.

But what about the companies where no one cares, ever? I have heard the traumatic stories of those who have lived through that nightmare. "A slow death," was the way one friend described it. Bean counters fill the executive offices, and Heated Blacksmiths rule entire departments like a concentration camp. The corporate culture becomes toxic. No one wins in these environments. Even the executives, owners, and shareholders who consider their pocketed profits a win are deceived. It is of no profit to gain financially at the cost of your soul and the well-being of others.

Even in healthy workplaces, I've seen unhealthy leaders create toxic teams. Personal power is maximized. People become pawns. It takes only one poor leader with little or no oversight or accountability to make life miserable for many. In the same way, one good leader can turn things around.

I was honored to play a small part in watching the bunker transform. The contact center was moved. Policies were changed. People were equipped and empowered. The operation moved to a professional facility with a customer-centered team and a healthy work environment. All because of one leader with the will, the plan, and the power to make it happen.

## Life Lesson: The Difference One Makes

*"For my thoughts are not your thoughts, neither are your ways my ways," declares the Lord.*
Isaiah 55:8 (NIV)

*Hearing that Jesus had silenced the Sadducees, the Pharisees got together. One of them, an expert in the law, tested him with this question: "Teacher, which is the greatest commandment in the Law?"*

*Jesus replied: "'Love the Lord your God with all your heart and with all your soul and with all your*

*mind.' This is the first and greatest commandment. And the second is like it: 'Love your neighbor as yourself.' All the Law and the Prophets hang on these two commandments."*
Matthew 22:34–40

Jesus focused most of His three years of ministry in the rural backwaters of Judea. His teaching focused on training a ragtag team of twelve, along with a larger circle of equally unimpressive followers. An uneducated fisherman, a right-wing revolutionary, a left-wing Roman collaborator, a shepherd. Jesus traveled to small towns and borderlands. It's certainly not a great business plan if you want to change the world.

The way the world works is all about power, wealth, and influence. Jesus should have at least centered His operation in Jerusalem. That was the hub of Jewish power. The temple complex was the moneymaker and the pinnacle of education. That's where influential young lawyers were made. If Jesus really wanted to influence His people, He should have leveraged His networking with Nicodemus. He could have gained influential friends and investors to assure His marketing and public relations had maximum impact. He should have chosen the best and brightest as his disciples, those connected to the wealthiest families among the ruling class. That's how the world works.

The world operates on a power paradigm. Those with authority, might, and resources leverage their power to dictate the daily realities of those in their sphere of influence.

Jesus did the opposite.

Jesus's operational model was focused on the potential of every individual, not their power. Jesus filled people with divine potential, full of love and grace. They organically spread the transformational power of Spirit to others. I saw it happen in my own family and friends after I gave my life to Jesus.

Jesus's paradigm is not power down but love up. As lives are transformed by love, they spread that love and grace everywhere they go and in everything they do. As that love spreads, families and communities are transformed. In the first century, the Jesus Movement even turned the Roman Empire upside down.

I look back at the clients I've worked with. The senior vice president who changed a corporate culture. The CSR who made the Nazarite vow and who brought love and light with him every day. These people taught me about the power of an individual to employ the Spirit and subvert the most toxic of environments—even in the bunkers of this world.

I pray every time I step foot in a client's office. I want to bring light and love in a way that makes a positive difference in the lives of others.

> It's Jesus's model for changing the world. It begins
> with one person loving God and loving those with
> whom he or she interacts every day. It begins with me.

Leaders can't change cultures and companies without the right people in the right places turning vision into reality.

## Front-Line Managers Make the Difference

I could tell Ian was a sharp kid the first time we met. He had only been with the company for a year before being promoted from a front-line position to managing his team. The senior vice president over Ian's team faced a revolving door of failing young managers, so she asked me to mentor Ian.

He was capable and ambitious, but when I assessed his skills as a manager and leader, I found he lacked the basics. He had never learned time management, organization, or how to hold a one-on-one conversation with a team member. The educational system had failed him, and his company had no role models.

Fortunately, the senior VP understood what was needed and was willing to invest in coaching an aspiring young manager. I had the joy of walking alongside Ian and helping set him up for success. Not only did he prove faithful and capable in his managerial role, but he was soon put in charge of greater things.

Remember the vice president of customer service who turned the aircraft carrier of culture at the beginning of the chapter? I mentioned that the key to his success was assembling and developing a fantastic team of capable managers. Corporate culture flows from the corner office, but the front-line managers are the cultural gatekeepers. They make things happen—or not.

I have observed that front-line managers hold the toughest jobs in the company. They know what it feels like to be a man in the middle. They live in the middle. They must inspire, motivate, and hold agents accountable to rules they didn't set and can't control. They know what works and what's broken, yet they're often ignored and their knowledge remains untapped. They have influence and potential but lack training. Many clients ask me to work with front-line managers because they see a gap in basic leadership skills that companies once took for granted.

One of the biggest paradigm shifts I've witnessed in recent years has been the lack of developed young talent. Emerging generations have been failed by education, are dependent on technology, and lack real-world experience. Owners and executives set the culture and vision, but a front-line team rises or falls by the capability of front-line leadership. We can't assume young managers have the basic skills needed for the role. Senior leaders and companies must invest time and energy in mentoring and developing young talent.

# Life Lesson: Training for the Trenches

*Start children off on the way they should go, and even when they are old they will not turn from it.*
Proverbs 22:6

I mentioned earlier my first job was delivering papers. I became a paperboy when I was eleven years old. Every afternoon I delivered the *Des Moines Tribune* to residents within a few blocks of home. On Sunday mornings, I was up before the sun to deliver the giant Sunday morning edition of the *Des Moines Register*. I was also required to collect customers' payments, count money, fill out a ledger sheet, and submit my financial report to management each month. I was responsible for customer support and making sure I put each customer's newspaper where they desired. I was running my own little business, and it taught me many life skills.

I sometimes wonder if my generation experienced more change in our lifetimes than any other generation in human history. I grew up with transistor radios, analog watches, and four television stations on a black-and-white television. I was in high school when the first computer club was formed. We learned computer technology on the very first Apple computers and RadioShack TRS80s. I experienced the dawn of the technological age and all the changes it brought to business and life.

I have witnessed diminished opportunities for young people to work and to learn basic business and leadership skills. So many opportunities began with my experience as a paperboy, bussing tables, and working in the fields of Iowa. My generation grew up walking beans and detasseling corn. I learned valuable life lessons in every job.

Our daughters didn't have the same opportunities as they grew up. Life had changed. We lived in a new suburban development of townhouses when the girls were about ten years old. The neighborhood consisted of young couples, older couples, and many single adults.

Many of our neighbors had pets, so we saw an opportunity. We helped our girls start a pet-sitting business. If residents were gone for the weekend, the girls cared for their pets after school and on weekends. Residents loved that they could support our girls and keep their pets at home. The girls learned about marketing, negotiation, responsibility, and basic customer support. I've observed other adults doing the same with children and grandchildren.

I recently spoke with a client whose granddaughters showed an interest in making craft bead jewelry and key rings. She saw a business opportunity for the girls. She invested in getting the supplies. She oversees the business. The girls are now selling their goods at local farmer's markets and craft fairs. They are learning lessons many of their peers are not.

God's instructions for parents to "start children off on the way they should go" isn't limited to lessons on morality. A parent's job is to set their children up for success and then launch them on the path God has for them.

Setting them up for success includes teaching and modeling life skills and leadership. I was not a perfect parent. I'm sure my daughters could regale you with many stories of my shortcomings. I did, however, launch two incredible young women on very different life paths.

I love working with all leaders, from executives to front-line managers. I've learned so much from the different styles of leadership. I love being the man in the middle. I have the opportunity to help leaders understand their customers and speak truth into blind spots. I equip front-line agents and supervisors with skills that will enhance their success—and not only success in business. If they apply the principles in the right way, it will enhance their success in life.

If I want to accomplish Intelligentics' mission, I can't hang out exclusively in the C-suite. I have to climb in the trenches and get my hands dirty. That's where I get to make the greatest difference for customers, team members, and clients. Strategy might be set in the war room, but wars are ultimately won in the trenches.

To understand whether leadership decisions actually work, you have to leave the boardroom and listen to the people living with those decisions every day.

# CHAPTER 7

# Lessons from the Trenches

It was World War I. On Christmas Eve 1917, an unexpected truce broke out in certain stretches of the German and Allied trenches. The miraculous truce was organic and sporadic. Enemies emerged from their trenches, exchanged gifts, shared meals, and helped one another retrieve and bury their dead from the no-man's-land in between. In one true story, a German soldier who had driven a taxi in London before the war ran into the Brit who had been his barber. The Brit offered to give his former German customer a haircut as a Christmas gift. The stories of men on both sides reveal the lessons they learned that miraculous day. They had far more in common than their commanders or the public cared to admit.

I've spent many hours in the trenches of business. We have more in common with one another than most of us realize. Let me share with you some of my favorite, most common lessons from the trenches.

## Escalated Customers and the Empathy Gap

The CSR came to her coaching session with her shoulders slumped. Everything from the look on her face to the way she moved told me something was wrong. I typically start each coaching session by gauging the emotional temperature, so I asked if everything was all right. It wasn't. The CSR was reeling from an earful of human temper.

I asked her to describe what had happened during the call. As in most escalated cases, the company's service system kept failing to fix the customer's issue. My poor coaching student happened to be the disembodied voice who picked up the phone on behalf of the company when the customer blew a gasket.

As we processed the situation, I noticed that the CSR had brought her scratchpad with her to the session. It's very common for agents to keep a scratchpad at their desks. They write the customer's name, account numbers, or key information on it. After each call, they cross off the previous customer's name to get ready to record information on the next call.

Her scratchpad had a long list of customers she'd spoken to that day. I asked her to recount some of the other calls. She smiled, recalling how nice one of them had been. She discovered she had something in common with another, and they'd made a sort of connection. There was an amazing change in her affect as her mind shifted from the one angry customer to all the others she'd talked to earlier in the day. I looked at her list and pointed to the last name on her page.

"Is this the angry customer?" I asked her. She nodded.

I took her pad and created a fold on the page just above the name of that angry customer. Then I tore that name off, handed her the paper, and asked her to crumple it up into a ball as I reached for the waste can.

"We're going to toss that customer in here," I said, holding up the can for her. "And we're going to choose to remember the other customers you've served today."

The number one training request I receive is how to handle angry and escalated customers. The service skill that creates the greatest struggle for customer-facing agents is empathy and apology.

Data from our SQA consistently reveals that escalated customers represent less than 2 percent of total callers. They are the exceptions. My coaching session with the CSR that day was a perfect illustration of reality. Of the eighty phone calls my customer service protégée took that day, only one of them was rude. When it happens, however, it takes up an exponentially larger share of an associate's emotional energy. It rattles emotions. It is unnerving. It's hard for most people to shake it off and keep it in perspective. The exceptional angry customer rules their heart and minds.

I begin training in escalated call handling by sharing a hard truth. There is no magic pill to make things better for the customer or the agent. There are principles for handling angry customers that can calm the situation and ease stress. First, we must cut through the emotion and understand the problem.

Let's return to the Holy Trinity of CSAT. The number one driver of satisfaction is resolution. Most escalated customer situations stem from a lack of resolution. The second driver of satisfaction is courtesy and friendliness. In other words, the customer wants to know that someone cares about their unresolved situation. Frustration grows with repeated contacts and a lack of resolution. Frustration boils over when the customer feels that the company doesn't care. Add to this dilemma the fact that the customer feels repeated contacts have wasted their time, and the third element of the Holy Trinity is triggered. It's a perfect storm of dissatisfaction.

The most effective approach to an escalated customer is what I've dubbed an *empathy-resolution statement*. The statement quickly and clearly addresses the first two drivers of the CSAT Trinity. It begins with an apology. However, I've learned from experience that people don't like to apologize. Many refuse to do to so.

Apologies are by far the most misunderstood customer service skill. People carry personal feelings about apologizing, shaped by childhood, family, and cultural systems. But CSRs aren't dealing with a personal situation. To quote *The Godfather*, "It's not personal. It's strictly business."

If Wendy walks into the room when I'm on the phone with a company, I'll tell her, "I'm talking to the insurance company." I don't tell her, "I'm talking to Linda." I'm talking to a business by way of their representative. This is precisely why some customers find it easy to let their anger spew. The customer feels like they are talking to an extension of the voice response system. They are talking to an impersonal, disembodied voice.

The most simple and powerful way to communicate empathy is an apology using some form of the words *sorry* or *apologize*.

"I'm sorry to hear that's happened . . ."

"Sorry no one got back to you . . ."

"I apologize this hasn't been resolved . . ."

I hear reps say *unfortunately* as a form of apology, but it doesn't communicate the same thing. The root word *fortune* means *luck*. When a customer hears "Unfortunately, your order was delayed," the message is, "It's your bad luck your order was delayed." That's not empathy.

When a CSR says, "I apologize that your order was delayed," the customer hears that the company cares and knows their expectations weren't met.

"Yeah, but Tom? This one time, I had a customer who said, 'I don't want your apology!' So, I think you're wrong. Customers don't want us to apologize."

On rare occasions, I have heard customers say, "I don't want your apology." In those cases, one of two things has always been true. In some cases, the CSR *over*-apologized. For example, I recently analyzed a client email that was four sentences long and the CSR apologized three times. That's overkill. In other cases, the customer's issue can't or isn't being resolved to their satisfaction, so the apology sounds hollow and insincere.

An empathy-resolution statement quickly provides the apology right up front, then immediately focuses on what the customer wants—resolution. They finish by stating what they can or will do to move toward resolution.

"I apologize no one returned your call, Bob. What I'm going to do is . . ."

"I'm sorry to hear that was damaged. Let me get a replacement on its way to you, Maria."

An empathy-resolution statement tells the customer that someone cares and that they are taking ownership for fixing the issue. It's not a magic pill, but it's effective at quickly communicating exactly what escalated customers want most.

The reason no magic pill exists is that some customers are unreasonable. Some situations can't be resolved. It comes with the job. When this happens, I point team members right back to Customer Service Rule #1: Do the best you can with what you have.

CSRs sometimes have to deliver bad news. Someone has to speak the truth the customer doesn't want to hear. Doing the best I can with what I have often boils down to how I deliver the message. Sometimes I'm delivering a message I don't personally feel. It's like playing a character on stage who is very different than me. Early in my career, I came to the realization that CSRs are voice actors.

## Voice Actors

Recently, I coached a Gen Z rep in a tech support position. Our SQA revealed that she consistently missed a handful of soft skills, including apologies. In tech support, most customers call because the services they paid for aren't working. Almost every call is an opportunity for an empathy-resolution statement right up front. My young charge wouldn't do it.

I discovered through small talk that she was involved in her local community theater. She was excited to tell me about her most recent performance. As a fellow actor, I used this as an opportunity to reframe her thinking about her job. I explained that every call was an opportunity to practice voice acting. Her employer hired her to communicate with customers and resolve their issues using a loose script. While certain elements were required, she could improvise and personalize the script so that it sounded natural and conversational.

I explained that most elements she consistently missed could be met if she scripted them early in the call.

Customer: Hi. This is Michael Black. Our internet has been down for an hour.

TSR: Sorry to hear that, Michael. Let me check into that for you. May I have your address, please?

Empathy. Ownership. Courtesy and friendliness. It's as simple as delivering a line on stage. But she hadn't made the connection between her love of the stage and the job she performed every day. She is quite literally on the business stage performing as a representative of her employer. But she was unaware of it.

I recognize an internal struggle within agents as I coach them on empathy. They don't feel empathetic, courteous, or friendly toward the customer. I find it sad when individuals don't feel care and empathy toward their customers. Most agents care deeply about their customers. Some do not. The truth is that they aren't being paid to feel. They are paid to communicate. Communication is a matter of what to say and how to say it on the stage of commerce.

Here is another truth: we all control our own voices. We control the pitch, the power, and the pace. With that control, we can manipulate our voices to communicate a broad range of thoughts, facts, and emotions. We can allow our voices to channel our raw emotions. We can also control our voices to sound pleasant, friendly, and personable—even when we don't feel it.

My mother was an only child. As her mother, Grandma Golly, aged, she began to call every night. Inevitably, Grandma would call at the most inconvenient times, like when we were all eating dinner. I watched both of my parents groan. I observed them roll their eyes in frustration. I heard them mutter to themselves as they walked to the phone. My siblings and I could see that Mom and Dad weren't feeling particularly kind or hospitable. However, no matter who picked up the phone, Grandma Golly heard a cheery, "Hi Mom!"

My parents used their voices as a tool to convey an attitude they weren't feeling.

We do it all the time. It's voice acting. It's customer service.

Once I worked with an elite service provider perpetuating the fourth phase of the Service Excellence Journey. I hired a professional vocal coach to work with the team. She helped take their service to heights I'd never seen before. She taught them how to control their voices and use vocal traits to channel inflection that people naturally like. Our client loved it. It opened a whole new world of understanding for them. When you're dealing with millions of dollars in sales, you'll take any little edge you can. Sometimes it's as simple as how a person uses the pitch, power, and pace of their voice.

In a similar manner, I've observed that a team's failure can be equally simple. As simple as having the wrong people together on the same team.

## In Cold Blood—Team Dynamics

As part of a team-building initiative, I did an Enneagram assessment of every member of a client's team. Afterward, I did one-on-one coaching sessions with each team member.

Then I met the entire team. We discussed their Enneagram types. We discussed how their unique mix might affect team dynamics.

I was surprised to find that the team had three Enneagram Type Sevens. Type Sevens are the fun-havers. They are the life of any party. They are very serious about investigating all the possibilities for fun awaiting them. In my experience, three Type Sevens on a small team was unusual.

As I raised this fact with the team's manager and described an Enneagram Type Seven, he immediately named the three Sevens on his team. Then he informed me that the three of them sit together in one pod. Over their pod, they hung a banner proclaiming "Fun Island."

I had fun with that team exploring the strengths and opportunities represented by their rather unique dynamics. That's the thing about every Enneagram type. There are no good or bad types. They all bring different strengths and certain challenges to the team. Type Sevens are fun to be around. They also avoid pain and conflict like the plague. In times of struggle, Sevens will not be engaged. You'll find them hiding out on Fun Island investigating novel modes of future entertainment.

While studying the history of film in school, I examined the classic movie *In Cold Blood*. The movie is based on the true-crime novel by Truman Capote. It tells the story of two men who broke into a rural home in Kansas and murdered an entire family. A psychological analysis of the perpetrators concluded that neither of the men could have carried out the heinous act by himself. In essence, the two men in a relationship with one another created a type of third person who was capable and driven to commit the crime.

I've seen the same paradigm at work in client teams. Personality and Enneagram types mix into a cocktail of negativity. Team members spur one another in ways that aren't healthy or productive. It's not a problem of bad people. It's a problem of the wrong people placed together at the wrong time on the same team.

When I encounter teams mired in mediocrity, I work with the manager to investigate whether team dynamics need to change. Individuals influence one another when they sit in proximity for so many hours. The impact can be either positive or negative. I encourage managers to put new team members close to those who are consistently top performers. Observing how it's done all day can be a great passive coaching technique. In other cases, managers find it best to separate team members who are feeding one another's negative attitudes or behaviors. In extreme cases, clients play fruit basket upset. They disbanded the teams to give everyone a new start. I've watched it work and everyone won.

I've also found that it's easier to train a new associate than to motivate a veteran team member to change. Veterans are set in their ways through time and habit. Some have understandably grown cynical after all the fads and initiatives they've seen come and go over the years. But change is certainly not impossible. Sometimes it goes back to finding the right motivation.

Fred was a veteran who was less than enthusiastic about our service excellence initiative. However, we also recognized that he had leadership potential. Fred was a gambler. He was highly competitive. So, we put Fred in charge of a friendly team competition. The goal was to improve SQA scores and the customer experience. Fred suddenly became a supercharged and motivated performer. He transformed from a reluctant doubter to a catalyst for improvement. It proved to me once again how important it is to identify what motivates people. We just had to tap into his competitive nature. We had to nurture the veteran's natural capacity to inspire forward momentum in others.

## Commitment to the Journey

Remember our friend Jerry? The one who thought that the Service Excellence Journey was a passing fad? The one who finally said, "I decided it was time to just do it?" Jerry is a reminder of why companies must stay committed to excellence. It's important to beat the drum of delivering exceptional customer service perpetually. Jerry's long-term resistance, however, is a symptom of a common corporate malady. At every level, individuals want a magic pill. CSRs want one to make angry customers happy. Executives want quick fixes to solve deep cultural problems. Reaching for quick fixes becomes a revolving door of failed initiatives.

This revolving door leaves reps confused, exhausted, and disillusioned.

Inspirational events and annual Customer Service Week celebrations can lift morale for a time. There's nothing wrong with that. We all need an occasional shot in the arm. Everyone can benefit from some fun and encouragement. Companies have even utilized our pilot projects to boost morale. There's value in learning what your customers think, the opportunities for improvement, and team training.

However, events like these are like cold and flu medicine. They alleviate symptoms for a moment, but they don't cure the underlying issue. Some team members in the trenches will be inspired and motivated. That's the way they are wired. Others will wait for the dust to settle and the next quick-fix fad to emerge. They simply see no reason or feel no motivation to change.

Once again, this became more than a professional insight. Over time, I began to see the same patterns playing out in my marriage, my parenting, and my faith.

## Life Lesson: In It for the Long Haul

*Therefore, since we are surrounded by such a great cloud of witnesses, let us throw off everything that hinders and the sin that so easily entangles. And let us run with perseverance the race marked out for us. Hebrews 12:1*

*Be very careful, then, how you live—not as*
*unwise but as wise, making the most of every*
*opportunity, because the days are evil. Therefore*
*do not be foolish, but understand what the*
*Lord's will is.*
Ephesians 5:15–17

"You will proclaim My Word," the voice said to me on that strange, cold February night in 1981.

I had my own ideas about what that meant. Some of those notions proved true; however, God wasn't kidding when He said through the prophet Isaiah, "My ways are not your ways." Sometimes God leads us on paths we could never have imagined, for purposes we could never have foreseen.

In the late 1990s, I spoke with an acquaintance named Kevin. We served on board at church. During the conversation, Kevin mentioned that he wished he were more disciplined at reading the Bible. He knew it would be a good thing. Like many, he just struggled to do it.

Kevin was a sales rep who spent hours in his car every day making calls across multiple states. I suggested an experiment. We would each read one chapter of the Bible every weekday. Then each day we would talk over the phone to share one thing we each got from the chapter. We agreed to start the next day.

It worked. It became a habit. We both looked forward to our daily calls. Then, Kevin and I began to share things beyond the day's reading. We became friends. We shared life during those daily calls. Struggles in work, marriage, family, and every other life issue have been part of our regular conversations for over thirty years. Those phone calls continue to this day.

Something else happened in the years since we launched our chapter-a-day experiment. The internet changed everything about the way we do life and business. Not long after the turn of the century, the blogging world boomed, and it sparked another idea. What if I shared my daily reflections not only with Kevin but also in a blog post? How crazy to think that I could write my thoughts each day and publish them for the world to read? What a novel way to proclaim His Word, in a way that didn't exist just years before.

I mentioned earlier that I've blogged my way through every chapter in the Bible at least twice, and I'm still going it. During the COVID-19 lockdown, I began publishing the blog posts as a podcast. I invite you to join the chapter-a-day journey. I proclaim His Word daily, like scattering seed to the four winds, never knowing where it might take root and how it might bear fruit. I don't preach. I simply share what the chapter has for me that day. I hope it prompts others to think and reflect.

I could never have foreseen that God's calling would lead me on a career path in business and in QA. His ways were not my ways. After years of evaluations, presentations, and coaching, I see that one of life's greatest lessons is simple and profound. Proclaiming His Word is not defined by or confined to speaking on a platform or behind a pulpit. It happens in countless ways. It happens on a phone call and in a blog post. It happens when I teach someone how to respond to anger with empathy and when I speak truth to clients. It happens when I hit the "Publish" button every weekday morning in the quiet of my home office and when I thank Wendy for doing the laundry every week. And I still get to do it on a platform and behind a pulpit on occasion.

The journey out of slavery to mediocrity and to the Promised Land of customer service excellence is a long one. It takes discipline and perseverance. Through learning, experience, and guiding clients, I've found that it's much like the spiritual journey I began at fourteen.

My career has been part of a spiritual journey that brought me to a rewarding role serving incredible people I'd never have met otherwise. Those journeys continue. The Service Excellence Journey never ends. Change is constant, new challenges arise, and new generations must be taught, mentored, and trained to meet those challenges. Neither does my spiritual journey end on this side of eternity. I'm in it for the long haul. There's no turning back.

All journeys, whether in business, faith, or life, eventually bring us to a moment of reflection—a moment when the noise quiets and the meaning becomes clear.

# CHAPTER 8

# The Last Call

It was the end of a long day of coaching. By the time I began to make my way through the client's contact center toward the exit, the office was eerily empty. One last CSR was packing up her things. Standing there in the quiet of that empty contact center, I was reminded of something I'd learned over decades of listening.

There's a moment at the end of every shift when the headset comes off, the lights dim, the monitors flicker to sleep. The last call has been logged, the last notes on a customer's account entered, the final courteous closing offered. And somewhere in the quiet that follows, we remember what all of this has really been about.

It has never been about the metrics, the dashboards, or the scorecards. Those things have their place, but they're not the heartbeat of our work. They're the instruments, not the music. The melody comes from people—our customers, the colleagues we serve beside, and the leaders who show the way.

## Foundational

At its foundation, this work and this life are about listening. As Jesus reminded us, true listening goes beyond the physical act of sound perception. He spoke of hearing something deeper. It's about hearing not just what's said, but what's meant. It's perceiving things that percolate in the subtext. It's about building systems and standards that honor both the truth and the human behind it. Quality doesn't start with a policy; it starts with posture—the humble willingness to learn, adjust, and serve.

If I've learned anything on this journey, it's this: Companies that thrive treat excellence not as an event, but as a way of being.

## Quality

Quality is not perfection. It's a pursuit to build one another up. It's the restless hunger within great agents and leaders to make tomorrow's call, tomorrow's meeting, tomorrow's experience just a little better than today's. It happens when we begin every call asking, "How can I best serve my fellow human?"

You can't fake quality. You can't spreadsheet it into existence. You can cultivate it only through honesty, consistency, and care.

## Measuring Call Monitoring and Quality Assessment

Call monitoring and QA, when they are done well, are a sacred trust. It's not an audit but an act of stewardship. Every recording, every evaluation, every conversation we review is a mirror reflecting both the strength and soul of an organization.

The best QA programs aren't about catching mistakes, they're about catching moments. Moments in which a team member went above and beyond, moments that teach, moments that reveal. When we measure wisely, we see clearly. And when we see clearly, the path toward excellence reveals itself for both those who lead and those who serve.

## Morale and Motivation

Metrics alone will never move the heart. People don't give their best because they're watched. People give their best because they're believed in, celebrated, equipped, and empowered.

True motivation is born in meaning. It's in knowing that what I do matters, that someone notices, that I'm not just a voice in a queue or a number on a chart. It's in a leader's encouragement, a peer's thanks, a customer's sigh of relief as they exclaim, "You just made my day!"

Culture doesn't change overnight. It changes through a thousand small acts of integrity, kindness, and accountability that build trust, one brick at a time.

## Thoughts for Owners, Executives, and Leaders

The view from the corner office can be deceiving in a myriad of ways. Numbers tell one story; reality tells another. Don't just read the reports. Be present. Listen to the people. Sit in on the calls. Ask the uncomfortable questions.

Servant leadership isn't soft, it's courageous. Jesus modeled it as He washed the feet of His team members, as He sacrificed Himself for them. Servant leadership means putting the truth ahead of pride and the mission ahead of ego. It means owning the bad news, celebrating the good, and remembering that culture doesn't flow upward. It starts with you.

If you want your team to serve your customers well, serve them well.

As the old saying goes, the best time to plant a tree was twenty years ago. The second-best time to plant a tree is today. Take the first step on your Service Excellence Journey today.

## Thoughts for Team Members in the Trenches

You, my friend, are the brand. You are the living, breathing, flesh-and-blood proof of what your company stands for. You turn promises into experiences, one conversation at a time. You build a reputation, positive or negative, one customer interaction at a time.

You have days when you feel unseen, unheard, unappreciated. I know you do. Remember this: Excellence is never wasted. Every time you choose patience over frustration, kindness over indifference, or honesty over convenience, you're building something far larger than yourself.

Don't underestimate the quiet power of a well-timed "thank you," a calm tone, or a problem solved with grace. That's the stuff that changes customers and companies.

## Three Things I Hope You Take Away

If I were to distill everything I've learned—from tens of thousands of calls and countless conversations—into just a few truths, it would be these.

- Excellence requires intention. It doesn't happen by accident. It's built through daily discipline and deliberate care.
- Measurement is mercy, not judgment. Done with integrity, it reveals truth, and truth is the foundation of trust.
- Faith and work are symbiotic. The way we lead, serve, and treat others is our testimony.

## How May I Be of Service?

If these ideas resonate with you, there's no obligation, only an open door.

I welcome you to join me on my chapter-a-day journey at tomvanderwell.com or by subscribing to *The Wayfarer* Podcast on your platform of choice. Just search for "Wayfarer" and my name.

I'd be honored to provide a keynote or workshop on the material in this book. At Intelligentics, we help organizations build cultures of excellence by combining analytics with empathy, pairing what's measurable with what's meaningful. Our goal is simple: to show you a clear view of your customer experience and to give insights that create a win-win for all.

First, consider a pilot project of our continuous improvement method. It's easy as 1-2-3.

1. An objective VOC survey tells you exactly what your customers think. You'll learn about their experience and your team's opportunity areas.

2. A one-time SQA will reveal how your team is performing in comparison to customer expectations. Not only will it reveal the opportunities to improve customer satisfaction, but it will also provide a road map for getting there.

3. A training or coaching event in which the data from the survey and SQA become a custom blueprint for improvement. This isn't generic service training that has no relevance. We have listened to your customers. We have analyzed the calls, emails, and/or chats. We will customize training to the specific skills we know will

improve your customers' experiences. We have the data to prove it.

I walked out of the client's contact center long after everyone else had left. I looked back at the empty stations in the half-dimmed lights and paused to meditate in the moment. I'd spent the entire day coaching every agent. We reviewed their data. We listened to the calls. We worked on specific ways to improve the customer's experience on the very next call.

The last call is never the end. It can be the beginning of something better.

Thank you for sharing this journey with me. Regardless of where this journey leads you next, my hope is simple. May your calls be meaningful, your leadership courageous, and your service an act of grace.

# About the Author

Tom Vander Well has analyzed over 100,000 business phone calls in his career. He is President and CEO of Intelligentics, a research and assessment firm that helps companies measure and improve the customer experience along with customer satisfaction, retention, and loyalty for over three decades. Listening to tens of thousands of "moments of truth" between customers and companies has given Tom a unique perspective on success in both business and life. Tom lives in Pella, Iowa, with his wife, Wendy—his partner in all things. He has spent over a decade as president of his local community theater and as a teaching leader in his local gathering of Jesus's followers. Tom and Wendy have two daughters and three grandchildren.